REIKI AND BEYOND

HEALING MANUAL

One Planet ♥ One People

by S. Jeanne Gunn

Turtle Island (North America).

Light skinned peoples come from the East - in boats with wings.
The people will have two types of feet.

One - like a dove.   One - like an eagle.
Dove - represents new freedoms, love and kindness.
Eagle - represents strength, technologies, war.

The Eagle will dominate the new world and the light skinned ones will claw at the Red Nations.
The Red Nations (Indians) will lose their lands and their spirits.

Later times - the Mother Earth has become sick.
The greed - dishonesty - the technology for the sake of wealth.
Loss of forests - clean waters - fresh air - technology and greed have ruled.

How will the Earth Mother cleanse herself of this sickness?
Rumblings from deep within (earthquakes).
Lack of food and famines. Dis-easement. Weather changes. Deserts.

The Re-awakening. The Original Instructions. The Legend. The Myth.

Reincarnated souls - the elders - the thunder stick stories, the memories.
Together, the teachings of the peoples of all the lands - learning to Honor the place upon which we dwell.

The symbol of the RAINBOW :
> Represents - All Peoples, All Races, All Religions working together.
> Harmony, healing and wisdom will spread through out the lands.

The Teachers are the ***Rainbow Warriors***.
> Peace, harmony, abundance for All is the goal.   The Golden Age.

Reiki - is my way of helping the Planet.
> One Planet ♥ One People is my goal.

Reiki is a personal direction, a personal pathway for whatever type of healing work is important to you.
Writing a book - photographing nature - raising children. Reiki is the healing part of you that is within your
cells, within your breath, re-awakening to the *original instruction*!

NOTICE:

The Reiki and Beyond Manual has been written to enlighten and awaken the Light within each of us. This Manual has been set up to guide students who are interested in the Healing of themselves and others through the initiations and attunements of the Reiki Universal Life Force Energy, which is the basis of all life. The attunement is directed by the Master Reiki teacher to the student, activating the forces of the universe within.

This Manual will help those wanting to learn more about Reiki and will help in making a personal decision about taking this direction. This Manual is a tool and guide in your study of Reiki.

This Manual consists of: Reiki I, Reiki II, Quantum Reiki, and Beyond.
Included are true stories and experiences giving you an opportunity to understand what Reiki has meant to others and the going Beyond.

Reiki III/Masters Degree - is a Teaching Degree.

Library of Congress Cataloging in
Gunn, S. Jeanne
     Reiki and Beyond Healing Manual: One Planet ♥ One People
     S. Jeanne Gunn

     Includes bibliographical index.
     Includes glossary.

ISBN #0-9643412-0-4

Printed by:
Merrit Press
2460 Pleasure House Road
Virginia Beach, Virginia 23455

Order From:
Grassroots Publications
P.O. Box 1734
Virginia Beach, Virginia 23451

®
**Printed on Recycled Paper
Using Soy Ink**

One Planet ♥♥♥♥♥ One People

ACKNOWLEDGMENTS

This Healing Manual would not have been possible without love, energy and encouragement from many sources. I am grateful to Reiki Master Helen Borth, who during a difficult time in my life, helped me to become aware of a light at the end of the tunnel. I am grateful for the many friends who throughout my life have been there when I reached out. To three wonderful children (Daryl, Dennis and Jennifer), whose love and encouragement have always been with me; to my mother Shirley who I can always count on; to my friend Brook who continues to challenge me on my pathway; to Charles for a place to work; and to Cyndy for her support and Native American background.

I am grateful to the **friends** listed below who wanted to be a part of this project and for others listed in the Networking Sources, all extending out Universal Love and creating a beginning of -
One Planet ♥ One People

I am especially grateful to my Spiritual Guides, the Angelic Ones, the Ascended Ones, and the Beyond Ones; whom have blessed me with their love, wisdom and clarity for this project.

I Thank and Bless You All ♥♥♥♥♥

S. Jeanne Gunn, Author

Written Contributions:

Helen Borth	Ruth Hutton
Larry Borth	Kathryn Jones
Marius Broekhuizen	Lucille Larson
Daniel Cunningham	DuLois Lee
Joan Essig	Debbie Rine
Lucinda Fury	Linda Schiller
Lyn Gaither	Brenda Stone
Jennifer Gunn	Stephanie Story
C. E. Hamblin	Archie Whitehill
Sheila Hamblin	Claire Zieman

THE COUNCIL MEETS

The Thunder Stick Story

The Thunder came.   The Elder spoke.
The council is called.
The concerned people gather.

In a respectful and direct manner they form the circle that will be the meeting. The elder enters, coming to the far side of the circle. He is holding an array of colorful decorated sticks. They are tied with ribbons: red, yellow, black and white. *

A story will be told by the elder, this day. One of great importance about our Mother Earth, as well as to all Mankind. It is a story of peace and healing, a story that will be handed down from generation to generation.

As the story starts, one of the decorated sticks is handed to the first person in the circle, starting in a clockwise direction. He must remember the first part of the story as the Elder tells it. It is his to know and remember and repeat.

As the story continues, other sticks are passed and each person knows that they are to pass on that part of the story that their stick represents. In this way, the story is complete. Many people carrying out a part of the whole.

I see Reiki today, being like this council meeting. Each of us who awakens the healing energy within us by taking Reiki and receiving the attunements, is being given a stick. We are part of the whole story. Together, all over the world in brotherhood, we can work in balance and unity, passing on healing to ourselves and the Earth. Perhaps, if we work together, we can achieve the prophecy of Peace for which our Native American ancestors have worked.   HO!

* Reference: (Medicine Wheel)

the four races of man: red, yellow, black and white
the four directions: North, South, East and West
the four archangels: North-Uriel, South-Michael, East-Raphael, West-Gabriel
the four elements: North-earth, South-fire, East-air, West-water
the four animals repr: North-buffalo, South-coyote, East-eagle, West-bear

One Planet ♥ One People

Dancing, dancing, brilliant colors and dragonflies
Winds of air brushing by, aliken to sea gulls in the sky.

Whirling, spinning, atoms doing their dances of light
Is this what the Reiki life force energy is like?

Standing still, going within my center, my trance
Reiki healing energies swirling around, created the dance.

Where Earth, Sky, Water and Fire, the elements we need,
Here on this Mother Earth, where brotherhood should be heeded.

Are we like the Wind Dancer, in our dance of life
Are we listening to the personal pathway, or staying in strife?

Wind Dancer

Reiki energy swirling 'round, healing gentle and profound
Joining hands and hearts with love, to bring the "life force" from above
Helping us to heal each other, transfers the healing to the Earth Mother!

Lumis

One Planet ♥ ♥ ♥ ♥ ♥ One People

REIKI AND BEYOND TRAINING CENTER

Our center's concept and how it works . . .

It is our desire to help guide the individual onto the pathway of their choice using the Reiki Life Force Energy. Reiki is not just hands-on healing. Reiki is a way of life. Whatever your career - whatever your way of life - the *endless source of Divine God energy is available*.

♥   Reiki helps you go within for Meditation and Prayer

♥   Reiki is using your experiences and working with others: sharing

♥   Reiki is a personal Attunement and Initiation

♥   Reiki is a personal Purification of the Soul

♥   Reiki is a method of tapping into the Divine Source of Energy

♥   Reiki is Service: to Yourself, to the Brotherhood of Man, to the Planet

♥   Reiki is a Beginning: into Evolvement and your Right of Passage

♥   Reiki is what Jesus and the other Masters conveyed with their service to Mankind

♥   Reiki was re-discovered from long ago and is ever evolving into the Beyond

♥   Reiki Alignment connects you with your Spiritual Guides and Angelic Ones

♥   Reiki does not interfere with any religious preference or background

We want to help you journey towards understanding yourself and understanding the energy fields surrounding all living things. We will guide you with your personal attunement/initiation connection, thereby enabling you to find the many secrets of life and your right of passage. From there, you have the opportunity to take this information out into the world. You will be healing yourself, and those around you by the presence of your energy.

Become the *Wind Dancer* in your dance of life. Join us for a training session, or sponsor a training session in your area.

TABLE OF CONTENTS

Healing Experiences throughout the Manual.

WHAT IS REIKI

Reiki, a Japanese word (pronounced Ray-key) meaning Universal Life Force Energy, originated in Tibet. This study and philosophy has been handed down from the ancient traditions of the Sanskrit text teachings of The Vedas. The Vedas are a compilation of scriptures which were given to the great rishis (wise men) many thousands of years ago. The oldest known existing text is 5,000 years old.

Tibetan Buddhism is a mixture of the ancient ancestor worship and knowledge about channeling energies. Within this study of Energy, a science based on the language of symbols has evolved; one of the branches of this science of symbols is Reiki. Reiki is one of the simplest, most direct and powerful ways of focusing healing energy. Tibetan monks used various symbols in different ways to deepen their meditation practices as well as to heal and strengthen the body.

The Polynesian and Hawaiian races of the "Huna" (meaning secret) religion refer to this **universal vital energy force** as "Aumakua", a symbol of light, the transformation of the consciousness involved, coming direct from Totality without interference from the self, pure information. Memory stories have been handed down from ancient times, Egyptian, Greek, Native Americans, etc.

Speculation based on knowledge of other ancient healing systems shed light on the Tibetan Buddhist healing technique referred to as the **Medicine Buddha.** Medicine Buddha involves the "laying on of hands", the ability of transmitting this healing method through "an empowerment" from teacher to student; this is similar to the Reiki method of attunements. The Tibetan Buddhism is the only form of Buddhism that uses empowerments.

REI - Spiritual Wisdom

The Japanese kanji REI means spirit, air, essence of creation; a spiritually guided life force energy. Takata indicated seven levels of meaning; we've interpreted these as the seven layers of our field of energy, from the foundation to our outer levels. For clarification, see "Energy and Chakra" section. Further esoteric research gives a deeper meaning to the REI, supernatural knowledge or spiritual consciousness. **REI** is the God-consciousness of all knowing, the Core Star, the inner beingness, the cause and effect, or what to do to heal the situation.

KI - The Vital Life Force

The Japanese kanji meaning power or energy has the properties to unlock wisdom and psychic ability. Examples: The Chi in Chinese (1st recorded during the Yellow Empire over 4,000 years ago,) includes thirty-two different kinds of Chi. The corresponding Aumakau in Hawaiian means the connection between the superconscious and the conscious mind. It means that pure information is brought directly from the Totality, the Center, through the silver cord. Ki is the vital life force.

Reiki - A Spiritually Guided Healing Energy

It is the God-consciousness, the All-knowing called Rei that guides the life force called the Ki in Reiki healing. Reiki is to be experienced rather than intellectualized. Reiki channeled energy flows into the recipient, whose entire system is then charged and revitalized.

Reiki balancing will help us to stop spinning awkwardly off our pathway. It will help us to find the " center" from within, which we all extend out to others. Reiki will help us reconnect with life, and put us back on track with a purpose and intent.

Reiki - Not a Religion

Reiki is not a religion, nor is it connected with any religious group, but it does have a built in spiritual dimension, where healing takes place at a God-Conscious soul level. This, we firmly believe, is the reason for Reiki's effectiveness.

Reiki - Unity Concept

We have spent many generations becoming individuals, while losing the concept of unity. Now accepted globally, Reiki has reintroduced the concept of unity and harmony.

Reiki - Learning About It

Reiki is <u>not</u> dependent upon one's intellectual capacity or ability to learn. It does <u>not</u> take years. It is a personal experience, an activation within oneself, a connectedness to God-consciousness. Reiki healing procedures use a unique symbolic language. Reiki <u>does</u> require an open mind, a receptive attitude. Reiki <u>does not</u> require a student to change their belief system.

Reiki - Harmony with Nature

Through the invention of Kirlian photography, we got our first look at the "Life force" energy, and received confirmation of its existence, an existence that the ancient Native Americans were aware of. They lived in harmony with nature, not in spite of it, exchanging vibrational information with everything around them.

Healing means to make whole, accept and love all parts of ourselves, not just the parts we like.

Knowing about our interconnectedness to all life and acting accordingly is the first step in becoming one planet ♥ one people!

HARMONY OF NATURE - MAN AND HIS GARDEN

I was newly embarked on what you would call the "spiritual pathway" when I took the Reiki I course. I needed healing after a painful divorce. What better way was there to heal than by taking a course on healing?

The Reiki course helped me to understand some basics: universal laws, giving and receiving, intention, reincarnation, limitation, strength and much more. It enabled me to reclaim my sense of worth. It gave me hope, a new beginning, a light at the end of the tunnel.

About two years later, I was intent upon taking care of the four acres on which I lived. I enjoyed yard work and had always done most of the raking; but hardly ever any mowing, and moles: what did you do about moles, except swear at them??

The moles loved my beautiful geraniums! The deep red geraniums that I had planted along the rustic fence by the driveway, made a beautiful backdrop, until the moles discovered how good tasting the roots were. Imagine my surprise as I stood admiring my flowers only to watch them slowly getting smaller and disappearing! When I took a closer look, I could see that the moles (the rascals) had eaten the roots off the whole row and that the plants were just sort of leaning there! Now I had to plant two more flats of geraniums and If I did, would the same thing happen??

I asked the advise of a spiritual friend who said that I should talk to the "King of the Moles" and ask permission to get the moles to stop eating my geraniums. I thought about it; I believed it. Then I decided that the moles deserved to have something to eat. So I asked the King of the Moles to please enjoy another part of the yard. I told him that if they went to dine there, I would not bother them. I also made it clear that if they insisted upon eating my flowers, I would take action. They moved! And we got along fine for the next several years.

Well, that saved my geraniums, but not my strawberries! I was fairly new at gardening, but had just read in the Findhorn Gardens; they grew crops in very rocky soil and worked with energy beings. Well, I figured, if it worked for them, it could work for me too. I had large red strawberries, but they kept disappearing. Finally, much to my surprise, as I was reaching out to pick a juicy strawberry, a baby bunny snatched it - right before my eyes! Both of us got quite a scare. I knew that if I wanted to enjoy the crops in my garden, that I'd have to strike a bargain with the rabbits. I told them that they could have all the strawberries, but the rest of the garden was to be mine. It worked out very nicely. I had asked the "Head of the Rabbits" if this was an okay deal, and I sensed that it was.

Then there were the gypsy moths.......but we'll save that story for another day!!

I have now come to understand that there is a mutual respect and a balance in the environment. I honored that by loving them, honoring their rights: not killing them. It is important to work together for what is best for man and beast. We are all Divine Source. We are all a part of the consciousness of God. We are all living on one large cell (Mother Earth). We are all a community. When we act towards each other with respect and concern, we shall all become one planet ♥ one people!

Jeanne

REIKI - WHAT IT MEANS TO ME

That saying, "You could have knocked me over with a feather," could describe how I felt when I actually saw **Reiki** in action. Although I have a strong background in metaphysical studies, I'm not beyond being pleasantly in awe of confirmation that something like **Reiki** does work.

Having seen **Reiki** in action from both sides of the table (being worked on) and (working on), I'm still amazed and warmed by the numerous stories of it's healing energy. I'll admit that when I first saw the word, <u>Reiki</u>, I couldn't pronounce it. Once I'd heard it pronounced, I didn't know what it was. Perhaps I should say, I didn't know I knew what it was. I say this because I came to realize it is an age old practice, known to many cultures, by different names. The Native Americans used channeled healing energy for centuries in medicine healings. The "Medicine Men", of all tribes, all over the world have "known" of its existence since time began.

It's not an accident that **Reiki** is pronounced, "Ray - Key", because it is indeed a "Key" to healing oneself as well as others. The "Ray" part you experience during the actual practice of the healing, you may experience the opportunity of seeing or sensing color rays as the light permeates the room.

My introduction to **Reiki,** came when my six year old daughter was experiencing a chronic problem with U.T.I.'s (urinary tract infection). I decided to take her for a **Reiki** treatment in conjunction with the medical treatment she was receiving. This really helped her to heal and resume the normal life of a six year old.

After her treatment was finished, I was also given a Reiki treatment. I was hesitant at first, I was after all, there for my child: not for myself. Trusting the **Reiki Team** knew best, I relaxed on the table and was delighted by the warm, intense energy that enveloped me when they began. I felt such love! I envisioned dolphins swimming in the air around me, their gentle bodies gliding over mine. They radiated light and love and healing. The whole room was bathed in a bright multi-colored light. I could have stayed there forever.

Afterward, I felt wonderful. Little did I know that more had been accomplished that night than I'd ever expected, weeks before, while at the periodontist, the x-rays had shown I had advanced periodontal disease. I was told I would require extensive "flap surgery" to remove the diseased tissue from my gums to correct the problem. I had already started the deep cleaning treatments and was set up for surgery. At my next appointment, my doctor was surprised at my progress and told me I wouldn't require the flap-surgery. The periodontal disease was gone. I needed only two sessions to build up the tissue of my front gums, something associated more with my smoking habit than my periodontal disease.

In the fall I took **Reiki I**, to learn the technique for myself. It was a wonderful two-day intensive that reconnected me to an ancient knowledge of healing and universal love. It literally opened my eyes. During one of the healing sessions, as I was taking my turn on the table, I realized that although my eyelids were closed, I was seeing through them! The idea came that we don't need our eyes to see, that we are indeed limited by the reality we place ourselves in with physical our vision. Maybe if we close our eyes we will experience all those realities.... and beyond!

Lucinda Fury

THE CHALLENGE

He rode the Thunder down from the sky,

> *And pierced the Earth with a Warrior's cry,*

The Great Earth shook with the Force of his voice,

> *The challenge was met, there was no choice*

Maasaw sat and tended the Fire,

> *Protecting the Earth, his earnest desire*

He beseeched the people to paint their faces

> *And hold fast, the Earth, from all their places,*

And Pahana rose, like the Great White Whale,

> *From the sea, in the East on a boat with no sail.*

He was bringing the Word we all waited to see,

> *And he ate the Thunder and became the Tree ...*

We laid down our arrows and planted our spears feathers down

> *And as we laid our faces against the ground*

We heard the Earth speak, in a gentle voice ...

The Challenge was met, we had no choice!

Lumis

HISTORY OF REIKI

The history of the ancient healing method of Reiki and its' rediscovery has been told by the Grand Master Hawayo Takata (1900-1980), and passed onto all Reiki Masters and students in the following manner:

Dr. Mikao Usui:

Dr. Mikao Usui was born in Japan, and re-discovered the "hands-on" method during the mid-1800's. Dr. Usui developed techniques and invent truths that form the foundation of today's Reiki treatments and teaching through out the world.

Unsatisfied with healing only the spirit, Dr. Usui looked around him and saw the sick and disabilities of the physical. Awakened, his search for the ancient truths formulated in his mind and his quest began.

Dr. Usui started his journey by traveling throughout Japan, studying at the Buddist temples and asking questions about healing. In his questioning of, holy men, it was revealed that they were aware of healing techniques for the body about which much specific information had been lost due to their gradual disuse. They were now concentrating on the healing of the spirit. Dr. Usui was allowed to study the sacred writings at each of the temples he visited. It has been theorized that ancient masters, including Jesus, were Reiki masters, practitioners of the healing miracles, we read about in the Bible and other Holy Books.

Dr. Usui thought it would be useful to study the teachings in the ancient language and was encouraged in this quest by friends. Dr. Usui learned Chinese and Sanskrit. In the Indian sutras, (written in Sanskrit), Dr. Usui discovered information for contacting the higher source. After a long period of reading, study and discussion with the masters, Dr. Usui made the decision to travel to the holy mountain of Kori-yama.

On the mountain, Dr. Usui set aside twenty-one stones - one for each day he would fast and meditate in total solitude awaiting the healing information to be revealed to him. Before dawn on the twenty-first day, Dr. Usui, was looking in the direction of the horizon, saw a light beam coming toward him at great speed. His immediate reaction was an awareness that this light had consciousness and was the healing power. Dr. Usui knew the information he had been waiting for was within this light.

As the light became larger, it connected with his third eye area. Dr. Usui's sight opened into hundreds of little bubbles - atoms of light - all the colors of the rainbow! As Dr. Usui lay in an altered state, he saw within this great beam of light the Sanskrit symbols. He received his attunement and was initiated into Reiki. Thus, the healing method that had been lost for thousands of years had been reborn.

Dr. Usui practiced and taught Reiki in Japan, until his transition in 1930. He attuned sixteen teachers, one was Dr. Hayashi who worked closely with him.

Dr. Chujiro Hayashi:

Dr. Hayashi accepted the responsibility to preserve Reiki and to carry forward the Reiki work. He founded the Reiki Clinic in Tokyo and kept records of the treatments given. The detailed records gave Dr. Hayashi the information for the standard hand positions we now use. It was Dr. Hayashi who created the system of the Reiki Hand Positions, the Degrees of Reiki, and the initiation/attunement outline.

Dr. Hayashi was aware of a pending war with his country. He knew that most of the men that worked in the clinic would be called to duty. He wanted to preserve Reiki and made the decision to pass on the teachings and the techniques.   He trained two people, his wife and Hawayo Takata from Hawaii.

Dr. Hayashi made his transition in 1941, after going to Hawaii to help Hawayo Takata establish Reiki in that area.

Hawayo Takata:

Hawayo Takata was born in 1900 in Hawaii. She was a widow with two children. Her parents lived in Japan. Takata's traditional family responsibilities directed her back to Japan. Before leaving on the voyage by steamship, she became ill. The pressures of raising two children since the death of her husband had taxed her physically. Upon arriving in Japan she was hospitalized. The doctors informed Takata that she had gallstones, a tumor and appendicitis. After resting several weeks in preparation for surgery, she heard a voice saying; "the operation is not necessary." This voice, spoke to Takata three times. She then asked her doctor about alternatives, and was told about the Reiki Clinic run by Dr. Hayashi. She made the decision to try this rather than surgery.

Takata received Reiki treatments on a regular basis for approximately four months. She was so impressed with the practitioner's knowledge and the results of the Reiki treatments that she made the decision to stay in Japan and learn this technique. Takata took Reiki I in 1936 and worked with Dr. Hayashi for one year as part of her training. She then returned to Hawaii to establish the Reiki work there. Dr. Hayashi initiated Takata as a Reiki Master in 1938, she was the last master Hayashi initiated before his death.

After working with Reiki for many years, Takata realized the need to train others. To pass on this information to the Western world, she devised a *value system* she believed was necessary to quantify the worth of Reiki. The only way she knew to show the "value" of the training was to charge a large sum of money, as the expensive is seen as desirable. This was how the original fee structure of $10,000.00 was established for a Reiki Mastership.

Before Takata's transition in 1980, she initiated twenty-two Reiki Masters. These original teachers have taught others and there are now approximately 1,000 Reiki Masters, with as many as 100,000 people practicing Reiki throughout the world.

Takata's Masters

According to the Reiki Alliance (support group of Reiki practitioners), Takata initiated the following twenty-two Reiki Masters in the ten years among 1970 and 1980. Below is the list. (A fee for membership is required to join the Alliance -- see Networking Sources.)

George Araki
Dorothy Baba (deceased)
Ursula Baylow
Rick Bockner
Barbara Brown
Fran Brown
Patricia Ewing
Phyllis Lei Furumoto (Grand Master)
Beth Gray
John Gray
Iris Ishikura (deceased)

Harry Kubol
Ethel Lombardi
Barbara McCullough
Mary McFadyen
Paul Mitchell
Bethel Phaigh (deceased)
Barbara Weber Ray
Virginia Samdahl
Shinobu Saito
Tayata's sister
Wanja Twan

Reference:

(Henry Crow Dog -- "Raindrops")

As I work with Reiki in my life on a daily basis, I have discovered I use this method more and more. I am often reminded of something I read from a dialogue of Henry Crow Dog in May 1974.

He made the statement in reference to the Ghost Dance and it's revival. Its true meaning was one of peace and unity for all people, regardless of their color, all peoples living in harmony. He spoke of bringing back a love for Mother Earth. He spoke of Mother Earth as a living spirit with energies like **Raindrops** making a tiny brook, the many drops making a stream, the many streams making a mighty river - bursting all dams. We are the first Raindrops.

This is very profound to me. With Reiki, I too feel we are like the first Raindrops. As more and more of us begin to use Reiki on a day to day basis, we will become the mighty river; flowing over all boundaries and limitations, to heal and nurture and create a loving harmony in all that touch.

Lumis

The above list was the beginning - twenty-two Raindrops started the flow.
Now, Reiki is storming the World.

Planetary Need for Reiki

Spirituality has increased and become more apparent in the last few years. Words that were taboo and hush-hush twenty years ago, are now what we call "household words". There is a sense and feeling of urgency by many peoples on the planet to "clean house"; to become aware of our actions and the reactions this is causing in our environment. The Reiki healing energy has been one way many people are using, to spread and escalate a healing in our behavior patterns.

The well-being of our planet (the only place we have to live) and we the people on it are what this manual is all about. Taking a step forward in our personal development and personal action for the good of all, will create a better you and a better world. One of the basics is learning who you are, learning about the environment around you. Some of the basics are universal laws. We are awakening to the realization that the messes we create in our life, are up to us to un-create. The learning process and how we react to it is what our spiritual pathway is all about.

The basic concept of the Native American's "Great White Spirit" was with the red individual in their every thought, action and deed. Honor, their word, their actions were most important to them. The Circles of Life exist and are viewed in many concepts today. Wedding rings, the tree rings showing the years' life of a tree, the circle of earth, sun, moon, "crop circles", body cycles, planetary cycles, the Medicine Wheel, all showing the everlasting evolving cycles of man. This is spirits' way of showing us that we are an ever-evolving species, with opportunities to flow with life rather than against the natural flow of life. It is our choice!

We are looking to assist you in your awareness and development to create a better world. We want to help people change the way they interact with each other and with other living things. Through Reiki you are making a unified connection throughout the world. Like Henry Crow Dog's raindrops, we are all connecting on a vibratory level, healing the body, the mind and our society.

We, at the Reiki and Beyond Center, want Reiki to be available to everyone. It is our inheritance. It was not a coincidence that Reiki was re-discovered. Dr. Usui was guided, as each of us is now.

Reiki and Beyond Training Center

A non-profit organization (Grassroots Research) was organized in 1994. Under this umbrella are the Reiki and Beyond Training Center, the Reiki Newsletter (healing experiences, networking sources, children's column, etc.), Reiki Open House (for practicing and sharing), Bodywork Massage, Great White Spirit Medicine Wheel, Women's Goddess Council and Visionary Quests and more.

The Reiki training offered by the Center is based on Dr. Usui and Dr. Hayashi's methods, and moves beyond for the needs of the community and the planet. Incorporated into the training are the following: meditation, beaming and scanning energy, the basics of the body and its energy fields, body mind facilitation, intuitive direction, ancient symbols, spiritual guides and angels, quantum perspectives, moving beyond time and space, and alignment with the Golden Light. A closing crystal ceremony and ritual will be performed.

On our Board of Council: A visionary healer who assists people in understanding what is happening during attunement, treatment, meditations and communications with spiritual guides. A Native American who writes children's stories, speaks with school children on Native American customs, leads a Woman's Goddess Council, and creates Native American Ceremonial Art.

The attunements given by this Center follow the Usui method, a special Tibetan attunement, and the Golden Light Alignment. These attunements have been audited by our staff, and the empowerment has been clarified.

Mystical experiences during the past few years have guided us towards the opening of our Center. The Council of Elders provides treatments and Reiki training. We have created the *Reiki and Beyond Newsletter* which is our way of networking with you. We have been guided in our personal choices by many beautiful experiences.

Reiki and Beyond Training Center Fees

This Center has also made fee changes for the Reiki classes to make Reiki more affordable. Classes are available at the Center (check for dates) or you can sponsor a class in your area (please call to make arrangements).

Reiki I and II:	$250.00
Quantum Reiki:	$200.00
Reiki III/Master	$600.00

<u>Note:</u>

For detailed information about these classes, please turn to section entitled: Reiki and Beyond Training Center at the end of this manual. You too can become a Reiki initiate or Reiki teacher.

WAKE UP CALL

There was a time when all the people of the Earth were One.
Black man, Red man, White man, and Asian were One.
One land mass, we danced the spiral dance
And clung to the Mother Earth and worshipped beneath Father Sky.

Then the cataclysm
The separation of peoples and lands,
We spoke no longer with the same voice
We breathed no longer the same breath,
Our hearts no longer beat
With the rhythm of the Earth.

Look to this day and see
That the Brotherhood and the Sisterhood has grown small.

Look to this day and see
Death and destruction and hatred.

The Earth Mother is crying out

The water weep
The lands groan and split
The mountains spew fireballs into the sky
The sky turns dark and looks away
The Earth Mother is crying out to you and to me.

Pandora

USING REIKI

Outline of How to Use Reiki and Why:

1)   Reiki allows the light particles (the Oneness) to enlighten and heal the part of you that is in dis-easement, is feeling bad, hurts, is traumatized or has developed crystallization - all of which causes the disease.

2)   Reiki is channeled energy. Energy that flows through you, directed by Divine Source. You do not use your energy, so yours' is never depleted.

3)   The practitioner (you), receives a healing as the channeled Reiki Energy flows through you to the client.

4)   Reiki is self-guided by Divine Source and works where the client needs it most. Reiki flows throughout the body on chakra pathways and fields or levels of energy. (Fields of energy and chakras are explained in detail in another section of this Manual). The Reiki energy nourishes the cells, organs, atoms, molecules, the very essence of all that you are.

5)   A release of emotions can occur (laughing, crying, happiness), when the Reiki energy brings about a dissolution of inner conflicts and blockages. <u>Definitions:</u> Inner conflicts are the thoughts and patterns of thought you have incorporated into self from experiences in everyday life. Blockages are the actual build-up of energy that forms in our body, the part we sense and feel as pain.

6)   Unresolved experiences from many years ago, and unresolved experiences happening now build blockages and crystallization's in the body. These experiences sometimes take over and dictate your life. Talking about a subject constantly or keeping turmoil inside rather than expressing it are ways of holding onto blockages that can form a dis-easement in the physical body. This usually happens over a longer period of time, because your body is given signals. These signals are to help you realize to let go and let God control your life. Examples of unresolved items that can cause build-ups are: divorce, legal problems, career dissatisfaction, abusive mate, relationships with children, parents, companion, financial difficulties.

7)   Dis-easement is the end product of excessive stress, fear, worry, frustration, unchangeable habits and rigid thinking. These stresses activate the nervous system and the immune system. This cause - effect from the mind to the body connection sets into motion the physical problems - what we would call Overload.

8)   The reverse is possible. If the mind created the physical problem, then the mind can undo the physical problem. Reiki healing moves through out the body helping change the vibrations, the atoms, the blockages. Reiki helps put the client back into a state of unity and harmony within himself and the universe. However, needless to say, the client is not off the hook! Reiki can be a quick-fix so to speak. If the client doesn't change any of the thought processes or identify with what caused the problem, the client will continue to create the blockages and put the problem right back into their fields of energy. Sometimes this happens in another area of the body, and

sometimes in the same area. Therefore, the clients responsibility is to take charge of his thought processes, make changes in his life and then the effects of Reiki will have created a healing.

9) Deep rooted illnesses (chronic) - The Reiki treatments will guide the body through a cleansing. Sometimes a reaction will happen in the body where the body may actually not feel good as it is going through the process - But Reiki is working. The body has accepted the Reiki, the reaction is the adjustment the body sometimes goes through in deep-seated issues.

10) Remember to say thank you for the blessings of the healing. This is an acknowledgment to Divine Source that you accept the help. Then be patient. When one has taken years to develop an illness, the illness may need several treatments for the client to let go of the "stuff" he has hung onto. I realize we are a "quick-fix" society. Change doesn't always happen overnight!

11) Reiki works on all levels, the emotional, the mental, the physical, within the mind, body and soul. You can start using Reiki after you have received your first attunement. The intention of giving Reiki will start the flow of energy whenever and wherever you are. You do not have to be in a meditative state to use Reiki.

12) It is important that you do not force yourself upon a person who does not want Reiki; and is not interested or open to healing. In this case you can allow yourself to send energy out for the best interest and highest good of that person, knowing that your intention is for the good of mankind. Insisting you heal is probably ego. It is not our responsibility or directive to force a change on someone who does not want or is not open to a change in their illness. Doing so is being judgmental and interfering.

13) The more you work with Reiki energy, the more you can use it in your everyday life. Reiki is not just "hands on". Reiki works when driving down the street and you see an accident, or an injured bird. Reiki works when you are around someone who is very angry and upset. Reiki works in the hospital, fishing, checking out yard sales, at the supermarket. Reiki works anywhere and at anytime.

14) Reiki is the Divine Source that puts our misqualified energies into right action. Remember when doing healing work: the intention, the love, the compassion is most important. Misguided intentions (ego) is interfering with someone else's pathway, it is butting in, being judgmental.

15) Case histories have been documented in Japan with Dr. Hayashi, and with Hawayo Takata. The book Takata's Story on Reiki by Helen Haberly has many examples. The documentation shows case histories dealing with many illnesses and injuries. Examples: headaches, flue, colds, sore throats, asthma, tumors, PMS, fatigue, heart disease, cancer, kidneys, toxic conditions, arthritis, etc.

ADDICTIONS:

Reiki helps people who have unwanted habits or conditions: i.e. smoking, alcoholism, overeating. These habits if over excessive are like poisons to our body. Reiki II reaches the subconscious and works on that level of awareness within our body.

REIKI GUIDANCE:

Reiki triggers the knowledge and memory that dwells within the soul (the impression of the individual consciousness). Your intuition plays an important part in giving Reiki (sensing, feeling, seeing). By getting <u>intune</u> with the consciousness of Reiki, you enter a state of mind that connects and works between you and with your individual spiritual guides.

You may feel intense heat or cold, tingling sensations, or "holes" in the energy fields. Ask your spiritual (Reiki) guides to direct the energy for the best interest - highest good of the client. The client will give you feedback on where the energy is flowing. Trust the experience. Allow yourself to believe you have been guided to work where the client needed it most. You will soon learn a physical hurt isn't always where the energy field requires the Reiki. Example: legs represent going forward in life, your legs can be affected by your first or second chakra imbalance. Work from a state of intent, love and compassion for greater effectiveness.

REIKI NO-FAULT:

Reiki is a God-consciousness, universal life energy force. It will not harm anyone or anything. It is always helpful. You can never give too much or even too little of Reiki. Short treatments are beneficial if time is limited. Example: headache, toothache, earache, stings, cuts or bruises.

Reiki works on house plants, gardens, trees, dogs, cats, birds, fish, your automobile, your computer and whatever you desire to send healing energies to. Reiki goes out into the universe to work with the government, countries, health problems, emergencies or disasters, storms, unborn babies, global situations, our universe. By using this energy, we are aware and helping create a better universe, a better environment, a better commitment to ourselves. We are becoming the mass consciousness that can cancel destructive forces, we can do anything, we can create anything, all it takes is remembering Reiki is Love, Compassion, and Intention.

SPIRITUAL OR REIKI GUIDES:

Appearances in spirit form, angels, messengers have been reported since the beginning of time and through out every nation. Man hears voices, receives messages, sees spirit forms, has prophetic dreams and has been privileged to encounter many miracles.

With the confirmation of all of this, why would man question and want to use only the physical senses he is aware of? Our seeing, touch, taste, hearing and smell are to work with our sixth sense (intuition). What about our intuitiveness? Our guardian angels aren't asleep, and neither are the spiritual ones who will work with each one of us; helping us to focus and move forward on our spiritual pathway. Reiki is a wonderful opportunity of becoming aware of your potential.

The great master Buddha teaches that "you are what you think, having become what you thought". In essence saying, that for every cause there is an effect.

My Fish Story!

We all have a fish story in our life, but this is really a fish story??
One day while cleaning out the small fish tank that belonged to my children; both of the little goldfish fell into the kitchen sink. I couldn't make myself pick them up. They were slimy and slippery. I kept pouring water on them so they wouldn't die, but I just couldn't pick them up.

I was starting to get panicky. I had been pouring water on them for forty minutes, watching my children's pets gradually dry up. Finally I thought to call a neighbor to come and help me. She immediately put both fish back into the tank. The fish weren't doing very well. Then I remembered Reiki. I proceeded to use my Reiki skills that I had just learned and visualized a beautiful white light surrounding the fish tank. I placed my hands on the fish tank and send the Reiki energy into the water and the fish. Soon they were swimming around and acting normal.

Normal isn't the state they are currently in. Both fish are now fourteen months old. They are so big, they had to be moved into a 10 gallon tank. They are very beautiful and still love receiving the Reiki energy!

Debbie Rine

Angels and More

When there is a great need and a deep desire for healing, then the Angels will help if asked. Only when asked does your loving angel respond. Also, we must consciously create the atmosphere for receiving such a loving response to our needs. My own specific need had to do with a heavy mucous condition in my throat. This had existed for years and I thought I had to live with it and the added annoyance.

The answer came when a group of us met for weekly lessons in meditation and prayer. After a prayer to be willing to be open, we were directed to mentally put ourselves into a favorite room. My room was a large expansive but simply furnished room with large windows from ceiling to floor. I sat in a large armchair facing the window while the whole scene unfolded. Outside the window I could see green trees in the bright sunshine.

Presently, a beautiful angel appeared before me smiling. All was quiet. The scene etched itself permanently in my mind. I wanted to remain in this relaxed state forever. The angel asked the exact nature of my need. I explained my throat condition and asked if it could be healed.

Immediately, the angel turned into a huge beautiful butterfly. "Yes, this is not difficult. Twist a medium size bath towel tightly, dampen it with water, and fold it into a curve the size of your neck. Put the towel into the freezer on waxed paper. In the morning, wrap the towel around your neck and sit quietly until the cold is gone. Do this each morning until the condition is cured".

The butterfly and the whole scene vanished. Relaxed, thrilled and blessed, I was back in the presence of my companions around me. This was my answer. I followed the instructions faithfully for eight days before my throat became normal. Never again have I been bothered with that condition. The healing experience and my gratitude are still with me.

Kathyrn Jones

One Planet ♥ ♥ ♥ ♥ ♥ One People

How Do I Apply Reiki

After taking Reiki First Degree, I wondered about its application in my everyday life. Wow, now that I have this wonderful information, how do I use it?

In fact, I soon learned that I use it everyday. For myself when I sense a headache coming, I chant to myself (Reiki, Reiki, Reiki) over and over. This vibration cancels out my headaches. I use Reiki when my children have fallen or are ill. I use Reiki when they come home from school and need my special Reiki Hug. When my contractor husband comes home with bruises and cuts from the job - again I use Reiki. I also send out Reiki healing when I am doing counseling work on the telephone.

I am also an artist and do Native American Ceremonial Art and teach classes on Dream Catchers. The energy and love I put into these items is sensed when people pick up the artwork and just can't put it down. This is a special joy to me, because I know I am connecting to many people around the world. My own little Reiki international.

Lucinda Fury

Waiting for Proof

I have a Bachelor's Degree in Biology with a minor in physical science and work in the inner city emergency room as a nurse. I tend to be a concrete thinker, methodology being the means. I am also a Christian. When I was initially introduced to Reiki, I had to analyze its implications, mentally dissect stories of its success and decide if it went against my religious beliefs in any way.

I was still skeptical when I attended my first session. The idea of putting into use a greater part of the brain, using scientifically proven electromagnetic energies was appealing. Plus Reiki is not a religion.

After the attunements by Reiki Master (author), better known to me as "mom", I started "seeing" or "sensing" different colors during the practice healing sessions. I prayed in the name of Jesus Christ to be certain these things were of God. I kept quiet about all this until several of the more open minded students began to discuss these same colors. I was totally astounded that I had "seen" the same colors they had seen.

If I had not physically attended the class, I would never have believed. Reiki is a marvelous tool for me at work. I have already used it to calm drug dependent violent patients, to comfort family members and to soothe frightened children. It has had an amazing effect on my professional practice and my life as a Christian.

Jennifer Gunn

Reiki Feedback

Most healings I had taken part in as a Reiki I practitioner were with other healers in a team effort. I felt they were skilled and had psychic abilities, and I, in comparison, was "just there" channeling the spiritual healing. I was assured I was doing my job well, they could feel the energy coming through me, or see my auric field change, but I had little tangible feedback myself.

A friend and I teamed up to do a Reiki treatment on another friend. Both were psychic and one was a visionary who saw way beyond ordinary eyes. Both friends told me that my energy was powerful and helpful. The client - afflicted with Lupus, told me how much our treatment helped relieve the tension and pain she was accustomed to living with. She had been able to relax and fall into a normal sleep, rather than run on nervous energy and collapse into unconsciousness. That was some feedback!

However, at the next session with this client I alone treated her. We had only fifteen minutes and so I treated only the upper chakra areas and her hand, which was the most disabled body part. The veins on the back of her hands and arms stood out noticeably. After I had worked on her arm and hand for a few minutes, she told me that the pain had lessened noticeably and she pointed out that the veins had gone down. I could see the difference. By the time I finished the treatment, the veins on her hands and forearm were barely noticeable and the limb looked more normal.

It was not the aesthetic effect that mattered to me, but the undeniable, visible evidence that something had changed since I started the treatment. A great feedback for me!

I have taken part in other healings, and have seen first hand healings with people who have burned their feet at a firewalk, and healings of emotional traumas. But this was a simple solo healing. This was the confirmation I needed, to know that the Reiki healing power of the universe flows through me since I was attuned to Reiki. And, as the psychic Edgar Cayce has said, "use that at hand and more will be given".

Danny Cunningham

Secret Reiki

My friend and I were driving together along the expressway from Florida back to Virginia when we came upon an automobile accident. We pulled over, both thinking at once; maybe they needed Reiki. There was no ambulance on the scene, just one policeman and a bystander who had stopped to help. The victims of the accident, a mother and her baby, stood by the side of their overturned pick up truck.

Apparently a tire had blown and the truck skidded off the road and flipped. Miraculously, no one was hurt. With my background in first aid and certification as a nurses aide, I instinctively reached for the blanket that I carry my car. My friend and I approached the young mother and wrapped her and the child with the blanket, holding it around them as she stood talking to the police officer. All the important details of clearing up the accident proceeded easily, and the ambulance driver drove away empty, due to the fact that the mother and child "felt okay".

My friend and I left the scene satisfied that using Reiki was a positive response in this situation. We had independently decided to help and mused joyfully as we drove up the highway, how these people had no idea who had "really" come to their assistance.

By the way, I took the blown tire as a warning to have one of my bad tires replaced. This I did at the next exit. There was a gift in this for all concerned.

Linda Schiller

Meditation and Our Belief Systems

Many of my experiences are with facets of every day life. In fact it's a way of life. It happens all time and it is related to everything. It relates to family matters, legal situations, personal problems, our health, everything.

I don't meditate for long periods of time. Rather, I would say I am some what in a constant state of meditation. This sees me through all of life. One thing that was instrumental in putting me into this attitude was Silva. In Silva, I learned the three-finger method (thumb and two fingers). By holding this position several times while going through the Silva course, we programmed ourselves to go into instant meditation. This made us focus immediately. It is extremely helpful. It is wonderful in a case of instant need.

Many years ago I burned myself on a toaster - or rather I should have burned myself, I did not. I had just toasted some bread and decided to move the toaster. Perhaps, I wasn't thinking, but perhaps I needed this very special experience. I simply lifted the steaming hot toaster. Somehow, I knew to pay it no mind, to go into an instant state of meditation and go on as if nothing had happened. Well, nothing did happen. Of course, the flesh turned white - flesh is material matter; however, never did it blister. It didn't hurt one bit. Before long the surface skin simply sluffed off and all was well. I remember telling my little daughter who was in the kitchen, when this happened to follow this method should she ever experience a similar situation; to go on as if nothing had happened, (not permitting any negative thoughts). I also had the experience of walking on fire (twice); we didn't get burned, it works.

Three decades ago, I tore my heart muscle. I could hear and feel the scraping as my heart labored to survive. I did not go to an MD, only had a chiropractor come to the house to release the stuck points (I do not necessarily advocate this method to others). I was very sick. I did heal and I healed well. I was told that I was lucky that this did not leave scarred tissue and injure my heart into the forever and shorten my life. I simply calmed myself, went into meditation and believed.

Five years ago, I discovered to my dismay, that I had a lump in my breast the size of a marble. I felt no pain and it was perchance that I learned of it. Being a believer I thought I'd tackle it my way. I went on a fast and meditation. I did not go to an MD and have a biopsy (again I do not necessarily advocate this for others). First, I had to finish my various engagements; this way I would not have to tell anyone of my plans. Talking about it may dilute the positive attitude. Tell no one, just go with it. Well, my fast lasted 23 days. The lump went down 50%. I sensed to fast longer without assistance wasn't wise. Gradually the lump went away. The lump could have been benign, I do not know, it doesn't matter.

I believe that all things work out for the best. I should not interfere, but accept, meditate, take a positive attitude and just go on.

Lucille Larson

Mass Consciousness vs. the Hurricane

We all like a good story about the weather. But this is a story woven together from different people and yet working as a whole, the becoming the mass consciousness.

Last year in a channeling session, a friend and I picked up that the Angels wanted us to be aware of the Eastern coastline. We decided we should send healing energy toward that area. We visualized the Angels putting beautiful healing crystals (violet ray - transmuting) into the water.

We contacted a friend who was traveling up the coastline in a few days and asked her to send healing energies along the route to the Northeast. Soon another friend contacted me, and she had been told by her friend that something was up with the Eastern coastline. Then another friend called and said "my guides are telling me we need to go down to the ocean and play, to have fun; because the water needs to be healed, the animals and the coastline".

Several of us gathered at the beach for a healing ceremony. We asked the Archangels from the four directions to be with us, guide us and help us. We had brought along candles, blankets, and sage. We danced, acted silly and sang. We had an enjoyable time.

All of this was a month before the concept of a Hurricane . . .

We all continued sending out positive thoughts, and later I learned others were doing the same thing. Soon we heard that a storm was coming. The TV news talked and talked about doom and gloom. Everyone seemed to be dashing around in a panic to get their supplies. I had one friend say to me, "be sure you have food - what happens if it floods"? I wasn't concerned. There was food and water in the pantry, and we always had candles and batteries. I could never understand why so many people waited until the last minute to rush around and get so upset and negative. I finally told my friend, "if you would spend as much time praying for the situation as you are with your hysteria, there won't be a storm. It is your attitude and panic that will build the storm into destruction." This fell on deaf ears.

The storm is coming. The storm is coming!!

Well, I decided to go to the beach and say a prayer. The winds were gathering intensity and clouds blackened the sky. When I arrived at the beach, low and behold a miracle. Hundreds and hundreds of people had gathered there. Riding bikes, playing, flying kites, surfing on the larger than normal waves, blankets and picnics; everyone was waiting for the arrival of the hurricane. This was really something, no invitations had been send, except by the angels!! We all waited in anticipation for the storm. The sky seemed to be getting darker and darker. Television crews had staked out their claim, run their long cables, and were interviewing the people.

Soon, not long after that the winds died down. The storm had decided not to attend our party. The hurricane according to the weather report had taken a sharp right angle turn, and moved out to sea. The sky started turning lighter and lighter. Soon the sky turned the most beautiful colors I had ever seen. A beautiful new peach golden coral color and what I called an electric blue. The clouds and the sky were magnificent. It was funny to hear later that several other people had also thought the blue was an electric blue. All of this showing a mass consciousness thought had been picked up by many people.

This was mass consciousness vs. the hurricane, we had won. I wonder how many people in Virginia Beach are enjoying the story and knowing they may have had a helping hand!!

I wonder if others, in other parts of our country or our world for that matter; if others would join with us, we could help change famines, sickness, disease, and other problems. We probably won't want to accept the responsibility that we have all created the problems, now its up to us to correct the situation.

Jeanne

ONE PLANET ♥ ONE PEOPLE

Warriors of the Rainbow, come listen to the Ancestors words

They will visit in sleeptime visions, and dreamtime dreams . . .

The Buffalo will come with the message,

    to tell the time of the Fifth World is near

Grow your hair, "White Eyes' Children",

    wear feathers and paint your faces

And speak of love as the Healer of the Mother Earth . . .

Seek the Elders' of the Red Race,

    and drink mightily of their wisdom

Changes are coming . . you must quiet your fears

Know the Warriors of The Rainbow Legacy are being called,

To walk in balance, so we may enter the Fifth World

    In Peace . . . as - One Planet ♥ One People . . . .

Mitakuye Oyasin   Ho!

Lumis

One Planet ♥ ♥ ♥ ♥ ♥ One People

WE ARE ENERGY BEINGS

Each individual is composed of a system of energy fields or auras which interact with each other and the environment. Our planet is a living universe; (i.e. trees, rocks, animals, water all have energy).

This energy known as the "aura" or "electromagnetic field" has been depicted as a luminous radiation surrounding the body. This aura has been shown painted in the traditional religions including Chinese and Japanese art, Buddhist and Egyptian cultures. In Native American traditions the aura was in the legend of the white buffalo. Descriptions in the bible illustrate the transfiguration of Christ using colors such as white and gold.

Each of our thoughts, emotions, and actions can be viewed as an energy discharge radiating from a localized source into the universal field. Our personal energy field or "self" as well as everyone else's personal energy field resides and receives, " nourishment" from this universal field. That is why on the inner levels we are all connected to one another.

If we think three dimensionally, we distort reality in thinking of ourselves as separate from everyone else in our universe. A person identifying with only the physical body, conscious mind and physical senses, and believing there is nothing more, will not perceive the universe as it really is, nor will he experience the relationship of interconnectedness, unity, the Oneness.

Scientists are beginning to discover forces that do not fit into the conventional Newtonian science of reality. Energies of the life-force are being studied by various researchers who recognize the vital importance and correlation of these to physical living systems.

Newtonian belief: human body is seen as a cellular mechanism.

New belief: human body is energy

 A new breed of physician/healer is evolving to understand the functioning of human beings - of matter as energy. These spiritual scientists are looking to the human body as the inner workings of nature and the secrets of the universe. By realizing that human beings are energy, one can comprehend new ways of looking at health and illness. In conjunction with drug and surgical approaches, vibrational medicine attempts to treat people with pure energy. Infinity of energy is the "beyond"" or the quantum outlook for the future of man.

Energy work changes unhealthy conditions in the human energy system, promoting a healthy energy field and producing harmony and balance. In this balanced state a human becomes more conscious of "self" and the connectedness of the whole; and is able to radiate energy from all of his centers of power and consciousness (chakras).

Central to the work of psycho-spiritual integration (massage, healing, rolfing) is the concept that the physical body is the outward manifestation of thought patterns (many from childhood), fears, and traumas that we have allowed to penetrate our energy fields. Within specific locations of our energy systems: sensations, emotions, thoughts, memories and other non-physical experiences are what we report to our doctors and therapists. Understanding how our physical symptoms are related to these locations will help us understand the nature of different illnesses.

Each energy layer appears different and has its own particular function.
The layers of the auric field are associated with a chakra (wheel of energy).

SEE BELOW: Fields of energy diagram
Seven levels showing - etheric, mental, emotional and mental as well as astral

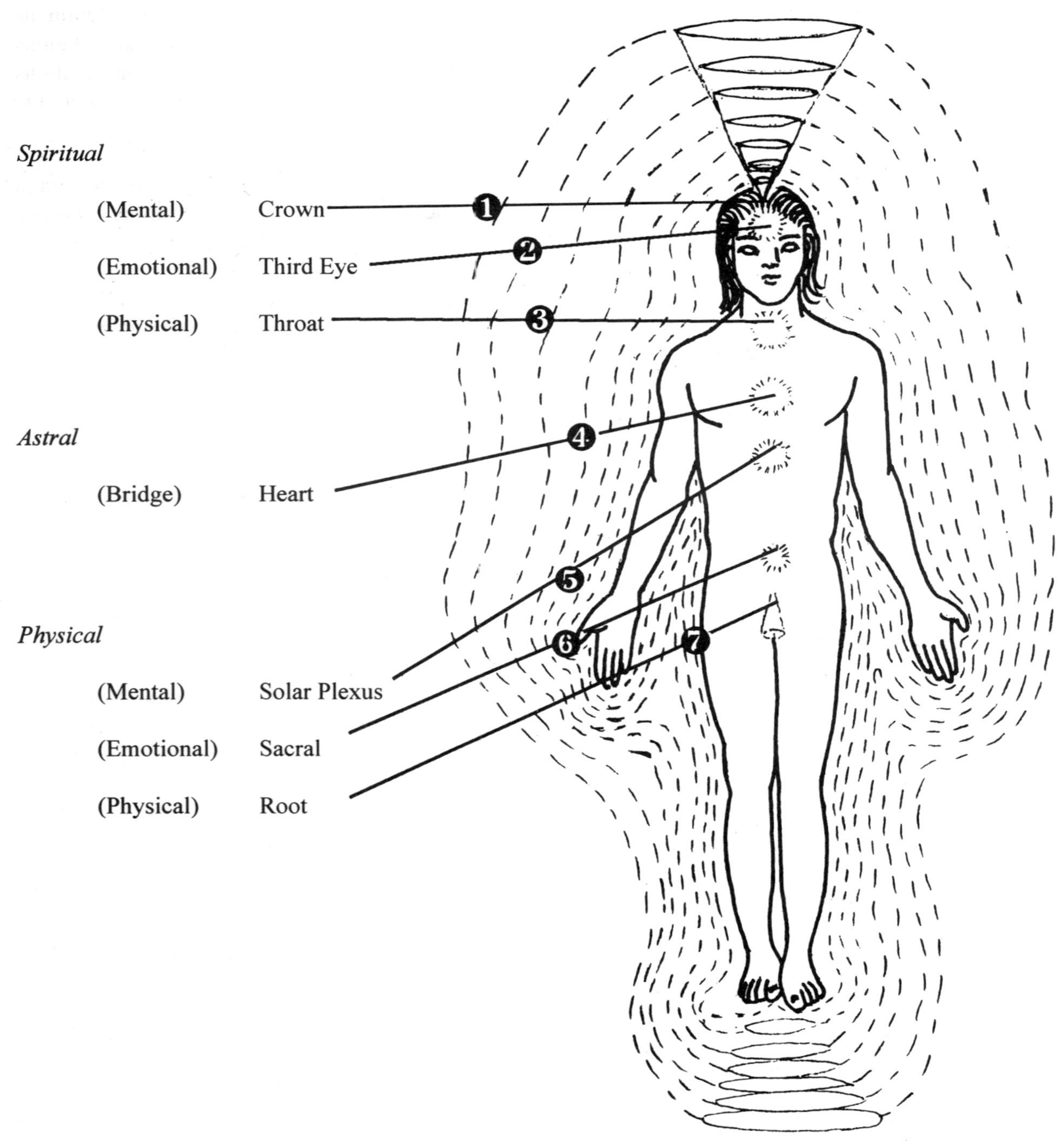

PHYSICAL PLANE

ETHERIC BODY:

(First layer) a state between energy and matter which is composed of tiny energy lines or light beams. The etheric body consists of a definite structure of lines of force or energy matrix, upon which the physical matter of the body tissues is shaped. This web-like structure is in constant motion. The physical tissues exist as such only because of the vital field of energy that is prior to, not a result of, the physical body. Field extends one quarter to two inches beyond the physical body.

EMOTIONAL BODY:

(Second layer) is associated with feelings. This field roughly follows the outline of the physical body. It's structure is more fluid (clouds of fine substance in continual motion) than etheric and does not duplicate the physical body. Field extends one to three inches from the body. This field of energy interpenetrates the denser bodies that it surrounds.

MENTAL BODY:

(Third layer) extends beyond the emotional and is composed of a still finer substance. Associated with thoughts and mental processes, it extends three to eight inches from the body. The mental body is a structured body. It contains the structure of our ideas. Clear and well formed ideas, produce clear thoughts associated with those ideas. Within this field can be seen thought forms. This is the level at which clairvoyants connect.

ASTRAL PLANE - BRIDGE

ASTRAL LEVEL:

(Fourth layer) is amorphous and is composed of clouds of color. The field extends one-half to one foot from the body. Interaction between people takes place at this level. Pleasant or unpleasant, you can **feel** the difference. People forming relationships grow cords out of their chakras that interconnect them. These cords exist on many levels of the auric field. When relationships end, these cords are torn and can cause pain. Many cords hang by strings if we keep reconnecting with traumatic issues like divorce, abuse, job related experiences, personal relationships, traumas, etc.

SPIRITUAL PLANE

ETHERIC TEMPLATE BODY:

(Fifth layer) contains all the forms (blueprint or negative of photograph) that exist on the physical plane. This grid structure is what the physical body builds on. The field extends out one and one half to two feet from the body. It is the level at which sound transforms matter. It is at this level that sound is most effective for healing the body.

CELESTIAL BODY:

(Sixth layer) is the emotional level of the spiritual plane. It is the level in which we experience spiritual ecstasy. Meditation, initiations, and transformation work, a point of being where we know our connection is with all the universe. Through it we see light and love in everyone and everything. The field extends two to two and a half feet from the body.

KETHERIC TEMPLATE:

(Seventh layer) is the mental level of the spiritual plane. The field extends two and one half to three feet from the body. The outer form is the shell (egg shape) of the aura and contains all the auric bodies associated with the present life an individual is living. It is composed of tiny threads of gold and silver (male and female essence) and holds the aura together. All the chakras and body forms appear to be made of golden light at this level. This is the strongest, most resilient level of the auric field. Its power current pulses up and down the spine, carrying energies through the roots of each chakra, and connecting the energies that are taken in through each chakra. The Ketheric field holds this present life's plan.

COSMIC PLANE:

The chakras above the seventh have been called the cosmic plane level. Some traditions have information relating to twelve chakras. So far most individuals have not connected with these energy fields.

CHAKRAS OR WHEELS OF LIGHT

"Chakra" is a Sanskrit word used by Hindus; meaning "wheel of light". Most traditions refer to the seven major (within the body) chakras and two outside the body (cosmic plane).

Visionaries (clairvoyants) perceive chakras as being circular spirals of energy which differ in size and vibrate at different frequencies. Chakras serve as gateways/portals to collect and take up the flow of assimilated energy into our physical bodies; our material bodies could not exist without them.

Chakras act as pressure valves for the subtle energy system. A blockage in the energy flow of the chakra or an excess of energy can lead to imbalance and disharmony on the physical, mental and spiritual levels. Our chakras react to every influence coming from outside, which in turn can draw together or open up the chakras accordingly.

A blockage is the build-up of energy that, when it reaches a certain saturation within each of us, causes a crystallization (pain). Examples: Shoulder pain often occurs when a person is feeling that they are carrying a heavy load of responsibilities. Ankle pain is associated with flexibility in thought and/or action. Lower back stress is often associated with stress over financial worries. Heart pain can mean relationship problems or worry about everyone and everything. Gall bladder problems are associated with anger or hurts. (You may want to refer to Louise Hay's book "How to Heal Your Body" for more information and for affirmation to assist in the healing process.

By breaking energy blockages, humans will again experience unconditional joy which is our birthright. There is spirit in everything, and its through this spirit (energy field) that the (I AM) makes contact and comes into relationship with everything in the manifest universe.

The seven main chakras correspond/connect with the major nerve plexus and glandular center (seven main glands) of the underline endocrine system. Lower chakras: (Root, Sacral, Solar Plexus) - correspond to the fundamental emotion and needs; vibrations are at a lower frequency. Upper chakras: (Throat, Brow, Crown) - correspond to man's higher mental and spiritual directions; and are of a finer energy frequency. (Heart Chakra is the Bridge through which all energies are processed.). One might visualize white light entering the crown chakra (prism) and flowing downward into different colors of the rainbow. Each chakra is associated with a different color.

Below is a diagram showing:
Location of the Seven Chakras (Wheels of Light)
Location of 21 minor chakra points

2 - sole of each foot	2 - front of each ear
2 - palm of each hand	2 - above each breast
2 - behind each knee	2 - gonad
2 - spleen	1 - thymus
2 - behind each eye	1 - clavicles area
1 - solar plexus	1 - liver
1 - stomach	

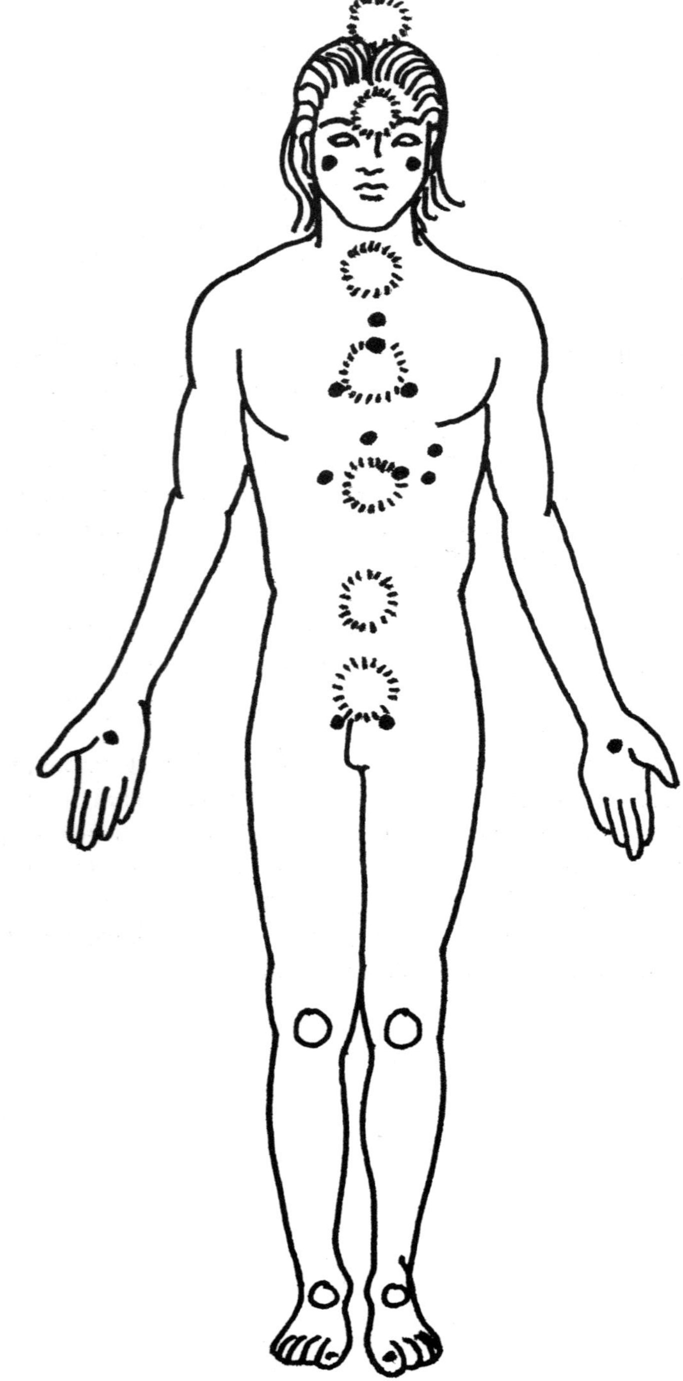

One Planet ♥ ♥ ♥ ♥ ♥ One People

CROWN CHAKRA:

Seventh: One of the highest vibrational centers in the subtle body, a deep inner searching (spiritual quest) for the meaning of life. Opening of the crown chakra allows one to enter into higher states of consciousness. A conscious activation represents the beginning of awareness of spiritual perfection or ascension.

Egyptian: KHABS: Divine, to shine through like a star, illumination

Linked with: the pineal gland
Location: top of head
Color: violet

Manifestation of Disease and/or Stress:

tiredness, weak psychic ability, cerebral dysfunction, psychosis, over wrought, creative exhaustion, migraines, nervous tension

Self healing:

Dance - move and experience the spirit of music
Writing, poetry, journaling, etc.
Vision quest or retreat into nature, sweatlodge
Light a lavender candle, relax, meditate

Crystals:
clear quartz, fluorite, amethyst

BROW CHAKRA:

Sixth: Referred to as the third eye or seat of intuition (clairvoyance), intuitive prowess. Conscious level of awareness, developed by various types of meditative practices. Also includes the person's concepts of reality and the universe or how he sees the world
Egyptian: KHU: Spirit Body/Spiritual, heart of light, seed of light

Linked with: energy polarity between pituitary and pineal glands.
Location: center of forehead.
Color: indigo

Manifestation of Disease and/or Stress:

not wanting to see something which is important to their soul growth, egotistical behavior, disorders of the nose, eyes, ears or sinuses, cataracts, arrogance, authoritative, obsessive, neurotic, headaches, pretension, loftiness and major endocrine imbalances, because of this chakra center's association with the pituitary gland

Self Healing:

Meditate, focus on indigo blue, go into the All-Mind consciousness
Visualize and activate your imagery - see yourself as completing your goals
Create a sacred space and burn incense.

Crystals:
azurite/silver - place amethyst on third eye area for soothing.

THROAT CHAKRA:

Fifth: Seat of intuition. Taking responsibility for one's personal needs. Center shows what state the person is living in with respect to receiving whatever is coming to him. An open center will attract nourishment. Clearing misconceptions of receiving or taking in, are transformed into trust in a benign nourishing universe. Center has influences over the major glands and structures in the neck region; including thyroid and parathyroid glands, mouth, vocal cords, trachea, cervical vertebrae, and parasympathetic nervous system. Key words: communication and expressing self, center of higher creativity of song and music. Known also as the center of the will. What way or how one communicates.

Egyptian: BA: Soul/Higher Mind: to shine, Be light, give light

Linked with: parathyroid and thyroid
Location: throat area.
Color: blue

Manifestation of Disease and/or Stress:

withdrawal, hyperventilation, hysterical, self concerned, possessiveness, controlling, dominating, fevers, respiratory problems, throat infections, laryngitis, coughing, rheumatism

Self-healing:

Chant. Sing, whistle, yell, scream, laugh.
Express yourself vocally in the shower, at the beach, in the mirror, don't hold back.
Lie outside in nature, look at the sky, breathe with mouth open
Fill throat with sky energy and blue serenity.
Enjoy some mint, spearmint or orange mint tea.
Write letters, write in your journal, write your feelings, your opinions, your advice, to send or not.

Crystals:
amber beads for throat and clarity, lapis for serenity, blue topaz for healing.

HEART CHAKRA:

Fourth: Bridge, center for connectedness and nurturing. Ability to express love, including self-love. Highest form of spiritual love Is unconditional love towards others. When this chakra Is in an open and loving state, you can see the whole Individual, the uniqueness, the inner beauty and the light; as well as the negative or undeveloped aspects. In the healing process the current power (energy) moves into the heart chakra before moving out of the hands, or eyes of the healer. The heart transmutes the earth plane energies to spiritual energies, then spiritual energies to earth energies for the clients use. Heart provides energy to bronchial tubes, lungs, breasts and the entire circulatory system.

Egyptian: AB: Heart/lower mind: Heart of the Soul, Heart's Desire, intentions, imagination

Linked with: thymus gland.
Location: middle/left of chest.
Color: green

Manifestation of Disease and/or Stress:

dissatisfaction, greed, envy, inconsiderateness, covetousness, imposing, coldness, blood pressure disorders, heart palpitations, ulcers, blood clots, itching palm, resentment, gall, bitterness, hostility, grudging

Self-Healing:

Be In nature, touch and hug a tree
Burn sage or thyme, allowing smoke to stream throughout house
Feel the peacefulness and change within yourself
Hug something, a pet, a rock, a teddy bear, a child, someone special
Take a walk on windy day, allow wind to sweep you clean
Prepare food requiring tactile work, kneading, chopping, etc.
Use scented oil to anoint your heart area. - mint, or lavender are good
Take time to be in the present moment
Breathe deeply, feel the weight of your hands, the position of your feet
Use a feather to cleanse your auric field, sweeping downward and allowing any misqualified energy to go into Mother Earth for cleansing

Crystals:
moss agates for soothing heart area
carnelians are stimulating
malachite earth's heart energies

LINK BETWEEN HEART AND THYMUS GLAND:

The term "thymus" is derived from the Greek word thymus, which means life-force or vitality. It is located in the middle of the chest, behind the upper part of breast-bone. Today we are aware that the thymus gland is the most important organ in the maintenance of our immune system. Researchers are now beginning to discover powerful regulatory hormones which are produced by this gland, influencing an individual's ability to fight off disease by enhancing the activity of different types of T-lymphocytes.

Various researchers have examined the link between emotions and illnesses and have found a strong association involving depression, grief and suppression in the immune functioning. Interplay of the blockages in the heart chakra may arise from an inability to express love, or even a lack of self-love. The ability to love oneself is far more important than many psychologists realize. Negative self-images, loss of self-worth, emotions of grief, sadness, loneliness, depression, and an inability to express love cause imbalances to occur with the heart chakra.

Medical researchers do not yet understand that the subtle energy flow of prana (life-force) through the heart chakra is an integral factor in the proper functioning of the thymus gland, thus the body's immune capability.

Individuals with strong immunology defenses may be able to remove virus from their system or limit its effects to minimal flu-like symptoms. A significant energy factor contributing to a strong immune response is a healthy flow of subtle energy through the heart chakra to support the thymus gland.

A weakened thymus gland can be strengthened within a matter of seconds. A wake up call to the thymus: tap lightly with your fingertips 10/20 times; this will stabilize your system and give you vitality. You can also Reiki your thymus. Strengthen your thymus on a regular daily basis and you will feel stronger. (Rubbing does not activate the thymus).

SOLAR PLEXUS CHAKRA:

Third: This is the center and issue of personal power whereby we relate to others in their life, express control over one's life, or are subjected to the whims of others. Issues of dominance and submission are the lesson. Viewpoint: Ones' sense of comfort with the universe as a nurturing place, as opposed to seeing the world as bad things waiting to happen. This center supplies energy to the major organs of digestion and purification; (i.e. stomach, pancreas, liver, gall bladder, spleen, adrenal glands, lumbar vertebrae, general digestive system). Programming into the unconscious mind during the early childhood years may manifest imbalances. An open solar plexus chakra will have a deeply fulfilling emotional life that does not overwhelm him. If closed he may not be connected to his own uniqueness within the universe and his greater purpose. This center is very important with regard to human connectedness. If connected he is firmly grounded in his place with the universe. He is the center of his own unique aspect of expression of the manifest universe and from this he derives spiritual wisdom.

Egyptian: KA Emotion/Desire: Image, genesis, character, reverberation

Linked with: major organs of digestion and purification (See list above)
Location: above the naval.
Color: yellow

Manifestation of Disease and/or Stress:

nervous dysfunction, intestinal disorders, energy blockages, delusion, exaggerated obsessions, abusiveness to others, aggressive anger, inner rage, depression, poor circulation, liver dysfunction, domination.

Self-Healing:

Go for a walk on a sunny, clear day
Read poetry that Is inspirational and soothing
Go to museums, zoos, places of pleasant joyful stimulation
See a funny movie. Laugh, loosen up, breathe
Make a nature arrangement of flowers, leaves, roots, stones.
Meditate, meditate, meditate and sleep
Do creative art, colors, textures - experiment visually; make interesting designs
String beads, focusing on each bead; use one color; forget patterns
Write out goals and achievements on slips, then burn papers
To release energies, burn during a waning moon
To attract energies, burn during a waxing moon

Crystals:
malachite is the most powerful; for emotional cleansing
malachite with azurite deals with subconscious memories
malachite with chrysocolla is for gentler cleansing

SACRAL CHAKRA:

Second: related to the quantity of sexual energy of a person. Open, a person feels his sexual power, blocked there will not be much sexual drive. The person would tend to avoid or disclaim. The nature of one's focus on sensual expression and sexuality can have both positive and negative effects; (i.e. over focusing to the exclusion of any higher spiritual pursuits, or creativity). Centering primarily In this chakra will tend to view relationships for their sexual and sensual aspects and to view people as sexual objects. A balance of giving and receiving, experiencing unity rather than separateness is necessary. The orgasm bathes the body in life energy, can be a holy experience culminating from the deep primordial evolutionary urges of mating on the physical level, and the deep spiritual yearnings of uniting with Divinity. This can be a wedding of both spiritual and physical aspects of the two human beings. This center is associated with the gonads, reproductive organs, urinary bladder, large and small intestines, the appendix, and the lumbar vertebrae

Egyptian: KHABIT Shadow/Etheric/Astral: Divine Shadow

Linked with: reproductive organs
Location: below the naval
Color: orange and peach

Manifestation of Disease and/or Stress:

repression, mask smothering, inhibitions, control, holding on to old relationships, lethargic, mental blocks, foreboding, worrisome, overly concerned, unfulfilled, lower back pain, colitis, kidney and spleen disorders

Self-Healing:

Take healing baths to soothe or energize:
Apple cider vinegar and epsom salts, this also helps clear toxins and cleanse repression
Drink healing teas: jasmine, hibiscus, chamomile, and orange spice
Drink water, water, water - flush it all out
Take a walk in the rain
Connect with earth and water elements
Fill a goblet with pure water, allow the sun to energize it
Sit in a warm shower with towel on your lower back - visualize tensions washing away
Take time for a personal party
Be silly

Crystals:
rhodochrosite-sense of self-confidence, self-peace
carnelians, jaspers and agates to energize and give courage.

ROOT CHAKRA:

First: is related to the quantity of physical energy and the will to live in the physical reality. Location is the first manifestation of the life force in the physical world. It reflects the degree to which we feel connected to the Earth and grounded in our activities. The ability to link with and function in day to day decisions controls basic survival instincts and primal feelings of fear from physical injury. Influence living in the present: I am here now and have the presence of power and vitality. Root chakra acts as a generator, a strong will to live. Too much energy this center: tendency to react defensively to most situations, can manifest paranoia, suicide, life is too much. This center is the seat of kundalini. A balanced center: Kundalini is the creative force of manifestation which assists in the alignment of the chakras; the release of stored stress from the body centers and the lifting of consciousness into higher spiritual levels.

Egyptian: Physical Body- Womb
                Generation of people, humanity, heart of the sycamore, belly of heaven

Linked with: sacrum, spine, rectum, anus and the urethra
Location: base of spine.
Color: red

Manifestation of Disease and/or Stress:

anger, frustration, insecurity, depression, lack of grounding, blood and nerve disorders, apprehensive, temper, lack of balance, suppression, lack of confidence

Self-Healing:
Weed in the garden; enjoy the fragrances of nature
Use perfumed oil that has earthy quality for you, rub on lower back and legs
Visual meditation - going into cave with the safety of your power animal for your journey
Work with clay
Sit with your back against a tree and feel the energy-earth connection
Lie in the grass, spine down - allow stresses to flow out of body into earth
Cry, scream, let go of built up inner tensions
Participate in a Sweatlodge ceremony for deep healing and earth connection.

Crystals:
garnet and red jasper for grounding
hawk-eye and smoky quartz to activate

EMOTIONAL AND SPIRITUAL CHAKRA IMBALANCES:

An understanding of how emotional and spiritual difficulties can create disease in the body is based on a broad working knowledge of how the chakras affect physical and mental illness, and can be the key to understanding and healing emotional blockage occurring in the body.

A healer can do a lot by simply "purifying" the chakras and balancing them out so that the energy flows.

Meditation/relaxation on a daily basis, visualizing white gold/silver light atoms of energy flowing upward (from earth) and out the crown chakra assists in maintaining balance. It is important to follow ALL the way through so as not to allow the energies to stop and stagnate at any particular chakra. You can also visualize the energies flowing from spirit into crown chakra and down to mother earth. Again, follow through. Saying positive affirmations relating to distress, or problems you are sensing within yourself is helpful. This is an energy clearing of your beingness. It helps to clear the mind of day-to-day concerns of the earthy personality, and allows higher information to be processed through the individual's consciousness.

HARA VITAL CENTER:

(Purpose/intention)

According to the Donning International Encyclopedic Psychic Dictionary by June Bletzer - **HARA** is the Japanese word for the vital center around which the whole body is centered. Our purpose and intent.

It is a laser-like line that runs down the center of our body. It is the foundation upon which our auric field is built. It corresponds to our life task or spiritual purpose. The HARA is visualized as a point two inches below the naval, running into the core of the earth, and upward above the head approximately three feet. According to Barbara Brennan's book, "*Light Emerging*", this is representative of our first individuation out of the godhead, the reason to incarnate in physical form, the place where we connect to our higher spiritual reality.

In doing healing work, when one centers themselves, it is to go to the core of your beingness, the HARA, and allow the divine essence to come through, letting go of anything within self for that moment and space. In doing so, the connection is made with the divine, yourself, the client; the energy flows in a positive constructive communion and the purpose and intent has been made.

INNER-LIGHT OR CORE STAR:

(Divine Essence)

Theory: All things began as one perfect light. Light is synonymous with intelligence. Each star is part of infinite. We are the center of the universe. We are One with the creator. We are divine essence.

An inner seeing shows people reflecting this inner light as a star, each one different, each one as an individual. This inner divine essence represents trust, faith, hope, encouragement, inner strength, loving, a deeper goodness. One might say, "they have a pure soul." From within this inner light, divine essence comes our creative energy.

The concept of natural healing is to use nature to fortify a weakened system so it can fight for itself. We can do our part by becoming aware of who we are, what we eat, how we think, becoming the spiritual being we really are; this is the balance and harmony.

Reiki - Inside Investigator

My daughter-in-law was having a difficult time with her pregnancy during the last few days of gestation. Besides the usual(I won't say normal!) complaints and discomforts, she experienced a period of 17 hours of labor with contractions at three minutes apart and no change in her cervical dilation. Her contractions finally stopped; partly, I'm sure, due to pure exhaustion. She was frustrated, scared and worn out. Her energy level was at the stress point. We decided some Reiki might be in order and put together a small team to work on her, the baby and the baby's father.

Afterward, she felt more relaxed and energized. She'd also received a massage to help with circulation and to work out tired muscles. After the father's treatment, they both felt more relaxed and able to cope. I felt strongly that the baby was fine, but a little apprehensive about being born.

The following week we found ourselves at the hospital. My daughter in-law's labor had been induced. After several hours of watching the various monitors hooked up to her and the baby, I came up with an idea. Would Reiki register on a monitor? The nurses had told me that the baby's heart rate should show a fluctuation, the more the better because it showed the baby was reactive. The baby's heart rate had been staying around 145, which they said was good, showing no stress. Should the heart rate drop drastically it would indicate a problem.

I started Reiki directly above the baby after brief scanning. I wanted to try hand placement for response. When I placed my hands in line with each other, there was very little response, as shown by a difference in heart rate. But when I moved my hands to a side-by-side position, the baby became immediately reactive! The monitor showed fluctuations from 145 to 159 and back every time I put my hands in that position. It was as if the baby was saying, "Yes! I feel that!". Later that morning we all got to meet our little "inside-investigator" face-to-face, a healthy 9 lb. 13 oz. boy!

Lucinda Fury

One Planet ♥ ♥ ♥ ♥ ♥ One People

REIKI MEDITATION AT THE BEACH

Start: Find a comfortable position.
        Relax.
        Breathe in deeply; exhale through mouth slowly. Relax and repeat, three times.

Envision yourself on a beautiful beach; you are alone.
The atmosphere, the place feels wonderful.
The sun is shining very gently.
The air feels smooth and silky on your skin.
The sand feels like a cool pillow under your feet.

(Sense all the vibrations of warm sun, cool air, soft sand)

You feel light and comfortable. Your body sways with the movement of the ocean.
Your mind is clear of all thoughts except for the experience of the beach.
Allow yourself a few minutes to enjoy it.

Now look above you. You see a beautiful swirl of lights in many colors, atoms dancing their dance.
These colors begin to form a series of colored circles. The colors are green and blue, blending in with
colors from the whole spectrum of colors. They blend and become one circle above you.

Now this circle is beginning to "funnel" down toward you, becoming many smaller circles as it drops
but they are all connected.

The energy of the "funnel" is wonderful.
It is healing and knowledge. Allow the energy to give you a message.
Bring the funnel directly over your head; bring it down through you.
Feel it traveling throughout your body,
Tiny colored sparks and atoms of healing energy.
Be aware of it filling your whole being, healing any part of you that needs healing.
Breathe in; exhale; relax.

Now, allow the funnel of energy to gently leave your body.
You may notice the color changes as it travels away from you and becomes a circle again.
As it goes outward from you, it becomes like the air.
Slowly come back into yourself, feel the beach, the sun, the cool breeze flowing around you.
Take a deep breath; exhale.
Return slowly to this reality.
Become aware that you are here and grounded.

Lumis

WIND DANCER

Now you see me, now you don't

I am the Wind Dancer, the dance in the smoke.

I am the power, the wind, mighty and strong,

I am the energy, of which you belong,

I am the song, the praises you sing

I am the Wind, beneath your wings.

I am your Spirit, I am your breath

I am the pulse that beats in your breast,

I am the breeze that blows in your hair

I am the warm fuzzies that keep you aware.

I am the dance, the wind of this dimension,

I am swirling energies of light, the mist - into ascension.

I am the Wind Dancer, the one in the smoke

Now you see me, now you don't.

Wind Dancer

PREPARATION FOR GIVING A REIKI TREATMENT

Your Role and Function - As The Healer:

Your function as the healer is to allow yourself to be a channel for the creative universal life energy flow, placing yourself in an unconditional caring mode, a non-judgmental mode; a "I AM" here to serve mode.

Your role as a healer is: <u>not</u> get involved in the curing process, but to be the liaison between the client and the creative force. Counseling may be involved, as well as giving information about vitamins, health care, alerting them to their body language, encouraging thoughts, visualization, etc.. These are all a part of the person who is facilitating the healing process.

Protection of Self:

In spiritual healing, the intent is first. A prayer of protection or affirmation is to be used for those without knowledge of the symbols. Visualize the Light of Christ within and outside of yourself, (being in a bubble of divine light above and below you. Use the "Power" symbol on front of body over the chakra areas.

Root your feet into Mother Earth, she is the nurturing aspect of the universe, you will feel the energy moving from deep down, moving upward and out the crown chakra, back to the heart center, out the arms and hands for the channeling work. Having your feet rooted or grounded, keeps yourself in balance in your work, always remember to see this energy flow either from roots to crown or from crown to roots so you don't block the flow within yourself.

Self preservation is the first cosmic law. We are all spiritual beings, but we are still in the physical body, and bound by the physical laws of the Universe. A prayer, the symbol, and an affirmation enforce your protection field to prevent you from <u>empathically</u> taking the dis-easement condition onto yourself. It is not our right to interfere and take on another persons ailments. It is essential to go within and ask for the Light of Christ to surround us and seal us in a protective shield while working on someone's energy field.

Spiritual Healing in Our Society:

When you are doing any spiritual work in your community, caution needs to be exercised when doing hands-on body work.

1) Clarification is needed as to whether a client is under a doctor's care.
2) Part of the healing process is to involve the family as a unit (in extreme cases, such as cancer, aids, strokes, etc.).
3) It is valuable to have information available about local organizations where the client may benefit from group counseling, funding, local herbalist, naturopathic doctor, and health food stores.

Scanning Client or Yourself:

Once you have received your initiation and attunement into Reiki and you are starting a treatment for a client, you will find that the attunement process has activated and increased your intuition and psychic energy.

After protecting yourself, take your *power hand (about 3-4 inches above body) and, starting at the top of the head, work slowly down the body over the chakra centers. Any distortions of energy, hot/cold spots, tingling, warm fuzzies, or having your eyes guide you to the spot where the energy field is moving irregularly, is where the Reiki energy is needed.

The more you use the Reiki energy, the quicker you will respond to any distortions in the clients' fields of energy. Do the treatment. Reference: *section* - Reiki Treatment Guide. The Reiki will heal the auric field of energy and the physical body connected to it.

Note:
Scanning for yourself is the same. Tuning in to your own body brings you into an awareness or consciousness of your body talking to you. Be as non-judgmental with yourself as you are with your client. Allow you to love you.

*(power hand is chosen at time of attunement by each individual)

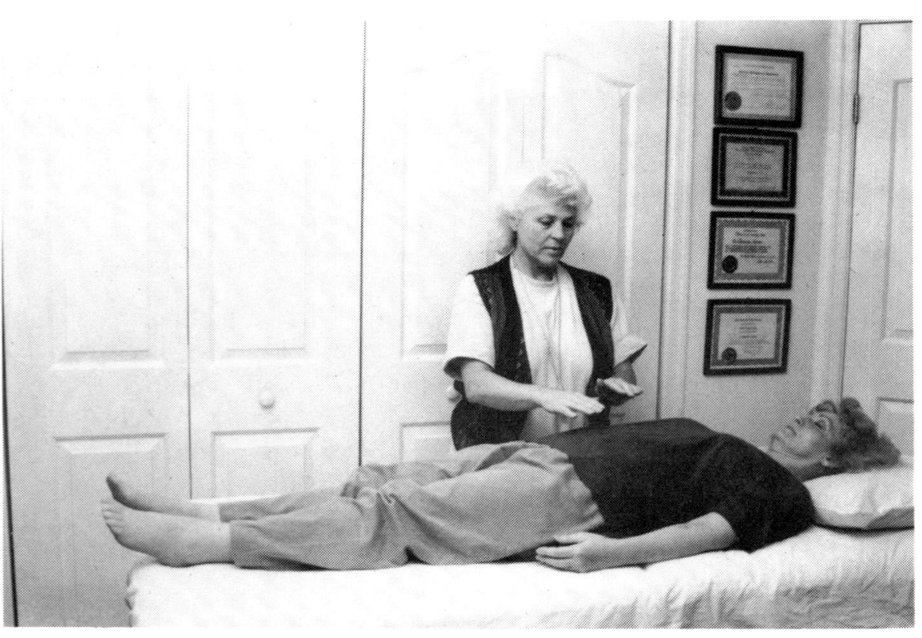

Radiating or Beaming Energy:

To **beam** or to **radiate** energy before and after a treatment, helps set the mode for the healing.

What is Radiating or Beaming? Protect yourself and then center your consciousness and focus. Hold your hands up and allow the universal life force energy (the atoms of energy) to flow forth. Project in a lazer flow from your channeled being to the client.

Keep your mind on the Reiki energy. Stay centered and focused. If your mind strays, bring the mind back to that altered state which allows the pathways of Reiki to flow. Having your spiritual Reiki guides work with you as you channel, strengthens the flow of energy.

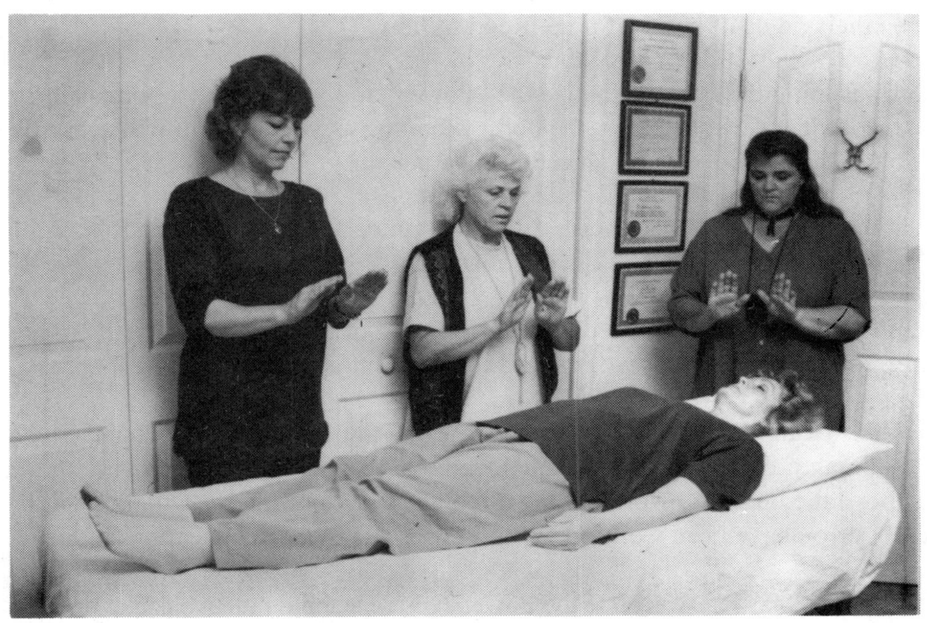

PROCEDURE FOR A TREATMENT

1) Before starting take the "Power Symbol and place this symbol either by direction with your hand, or visualize it on the wall in the treatment room. Burning incense or sage neutralizes the energies. A prayer to your spiritual guides, angels and the healing forces of the universe to work with you and with the client for their best interest and highest good.

2) Be sure your hands are washed to the elbows, before and after treatment. Prepare yourself by placing the "Power Symbol" up the front of the body over the chakra areas; and in the palm of each hand.

3) Talk to the client and have them fill out an information form. This gives you a basis to start from. A good connection between the practitioner and the client brings about a better focus for the energy to work.

4) You can direct the client's intention. Have them picture for themselves, what their problem looks like, smells like, what its' shape is, and what its' texture is. Saying a prayer of thankfulness, helps open their fields of energy for the Reiki to flow.

5) Before scanning the body, visualize the "Power" and "Mental" symbols over the client's body. Then take your hands gently down the body, scanning as you go. You will sense, feel, (sometimes heat or cold) areas where there is a need for healing.

6) Do the treatment, (Refer to Reiki Treatment guide for any of the body's problems as well as Reiki Facilitated Body Mind Work in this manual.

7) Beaming Reiki energy from a distance at the end of a treatment, helps facilitate a finalization. It also allows the consciousness to realize the treatment is over.

8) After the treatment, always close the rhythm, the vibrational frequencies and the fields of energy by doing a closing procedure of ruffling and smoothing. Then using the infinity symbol, starting above the head and working down the body and past the feet shake your hands, letting go of the energy you have been working with. This is part of a disconnection.

9) After the client has left, visualize the Power symbol again on the walls and the center of the room. This is done to clear energies worked on with the client. Burning incense, sage or spraying crystallized water, will reactivate and re-energize the room.

10) Thank the spiritual guides or angelic ones for helping the work for you and the client.

CLOSURE:

We have found the following to be extremely beneficial:

a) Gently smooth the **energy field** from above the top of head down to the feet - a ruffling effect.

b) Starting at the top of the head working down to the feet, make large circular motions. Bring the energy in towards the spine. Work slowly and finish at the feet in two or three circular motions, shaking your hands when finished as a cut off. Do this three times.

c) Using the figure 8 (infinity - yin/yang - male/female) starting above the head, work your way down the body. Visualize the weaving of a silver and gold thread as you do this, weaving the body's auric field back together.

d) Be sure to wash your hands to the elbows when finished. This helps to neutralize the energy you have been working with.

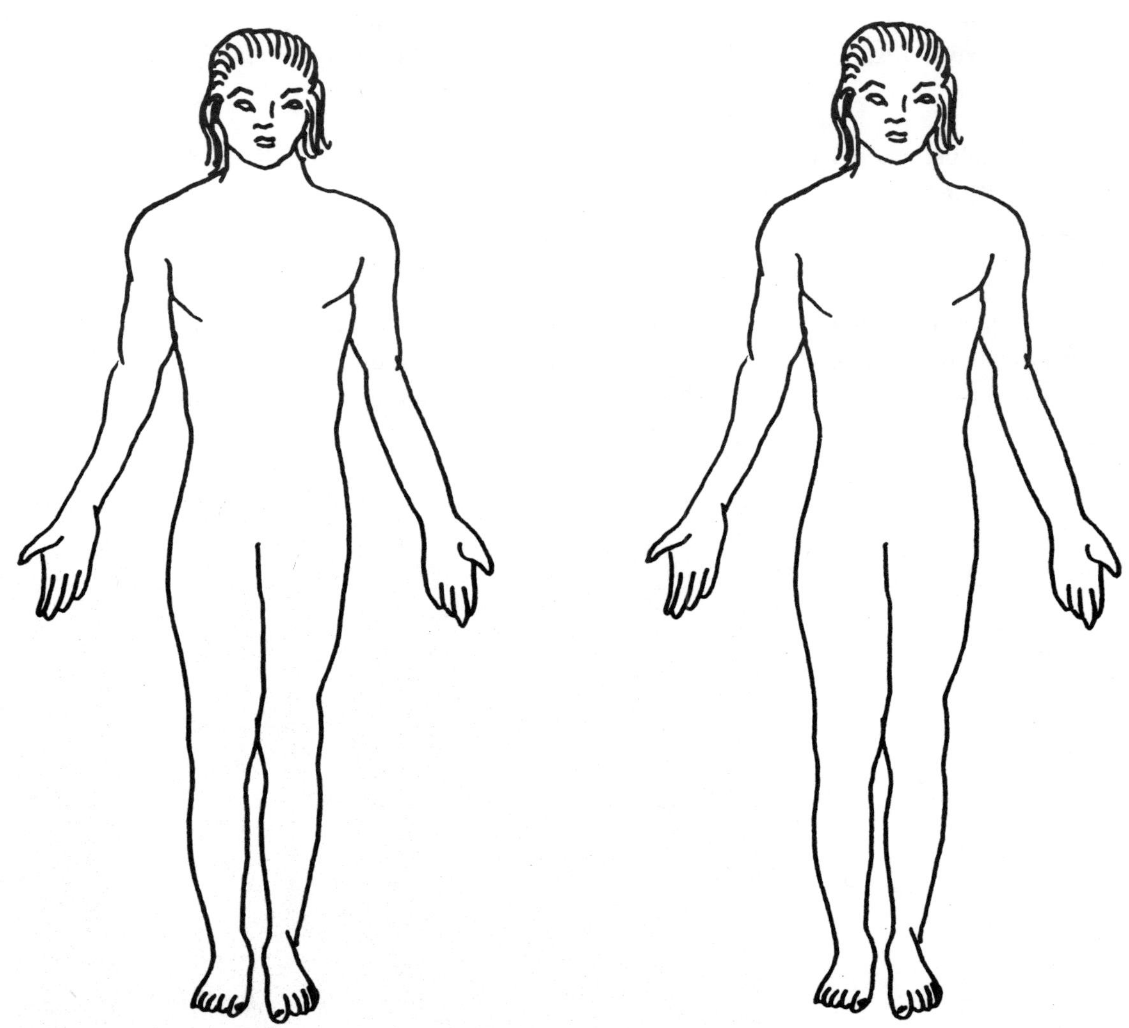

TIPS FOR HEALING:

Thought forms that **crystallized** in the physical body are the dis-easements that need healing. Counseling may be needed to connect to the source of thought forms that have produced the ailments. Being a practitioner of the healing arts its important to keep in mind at all times that it is the client's focus that has created this. The following may facilitate the client's awareness:

1) The client must want to let go of the condition on the conscious level. The client may reject healing if they are not ready to let go on a subconscious level.

2) The practitioner can help the client recognize how the ailment or dis-easement has served them, why they may have manifested the ailment, and that they now are aware of how they can let go of the limiting thought and action.

3) Clients need to identify with a thought pattern, accepting that the lesson is learned for their own soul growth, and accepting they are not physically or even emotionally responsible for another person's direction, life, actions, etc.(sometimes identified as karma).

4) Relationships between child and parent, between male and female, between friends, between greed, between dishonesty and control, all form crystallization's in the physical body due to limiting views.

5) Counseling clients that all things are possible to those who believe. Know that hope and miracles are within your grasp.

Dis-easement lives in unforgiveness. Forgiving and releasing resentments will help to dissolve the crystallizations we have built up in our body, even aids and cancer. If internal changes are not made, the disease will either come back or we will create another dis-easement.

FEARS - HOW THEY AFFECT US!!

DENIAL:
(Masking Self) We have created a mask of what we think the world would accept, thereby hiding emotional pain.   Many times this lies within the subconsciousness of our mind. This mask succeeds in giving us an inner feeling of security or safety, gives us the feeling we are the good guys, being critical of others, being afraid, fearful, putting constant pressure on ourselves to produce, not wanting to accept responsibility for our own actions.

Why? Why, have we created our denial, our mask, that has formed blocks in our auric field?

Examples of Masking Self:

a) Someone who has gone through a very traumatic event in younger years. This will sometimes provide a mask to others that everything is always okay, fine and they are in control when underneath they have a feeling of guilt, unworthiness, relationship problems, control.   Some people may actually be aggressive or fearful, while others will become the shadow where they do not want to be seen

b) When in everyday life you have to carry a lot of responsibility such as raising children by yourself, you will appear to have lots of strength and assertiveness, when underneath you really want to cry

c) A sense of abandonment, either from an early divorce in the family, being adopted, or the separation of parents, can cause many people to have relationship problems. They may have a sense of rejection, unworthiness, be overweight, be aggressive or have a lack of assertiveness, portrayed by their masks

d) We are in a period of time when the word co-dependent has been used for almost every family. It has helped bring this subject to the light, for almost everyone of us has had some drama we were masking - to what extent depends upon how we want to deal with the everyday world and life in general. Some people use the dramas they have grown up with as excuses for why they act the way they do, rather than changing the way they act. We are a generation wanting someone else to be responsible for all of our actions.

Masks:
being put down can cause - overachievers, aggressiveness
seeing family members cheat - gives you an excuse to be dishonest
work habits or role models - an excuse to look the other way, rather than be honorable
hearing dad degrade mom - you mask and act out against women
hearing mom gripe about dad - you may decide not to marry or have relationship problems
beings raised with beatings - that since you were beaten, anger causes you to beat others

What's Behind our Fears*:*

Luke 8:50 *"Fear not; believe only and you shall be made whole."*

Men of science have discovered Matter is composed of energy and information (quantum physics). That the universe and everything in it are of thought (God and God in action?); and that by observing and attention we are literally bringing into being particles from this infinite quantum field.

Wherever we put our attention, we draw things into being from this infinite universe of energy and information. Where we put our focus consistently causes conditions, situations, events and people into our lives. If our attention is positive (love, kindness, peace, balance and harmony); we can then create the coincidences to inform us of our outstanding question! If our attention is negative, that is also what we will draw into our lives.

Being part of the field of unified energy (oneness) is a way of defining your spiritual reality. Being always and forever connected and part of the endless divine god infinity creates the possibilities of abundance, peace, love, truth beauty, health, etc.; the fulfillment of life. All is ours and nothing keeps this from us; EXCEPT: <u>attention</u>, <u>belief</u>, <u>judging</u>, <u>uncertainty</u>, <u>frustration</u>, <u>anger</u>, <u>envy</u>, <u>condemning</u>, <u>impatience</u>, (our shadows). We have stepped from the Light into Darkness (from positive to negative).

Our thoughts draw blessings or burdens from our life situations, but the <u>attention</u> creates chemical messages (neuropeptides) in our bodies. These messages go straight to the heart of each cell with instruction of life, health, sadness or sickness. The tragedy is that knowing we exist in this unified field of infinite possibilities and unlimited abundance; we still create a hunger (a need) for security and assurances.

Jesus the master of Christ Consciousness taught abundance, he insisted that unbelievable power would be ours if we would/could believe. His demonstration that all good could be ours by multiplying the loaves and fishes, some saw this as lack and madness rather than God's unlimited possibilities.

Here's a story of an adept (student) going into forest and talking to his spiritual master, and asking "I want unlimited wealth, and I want to help heal the world". Please tell me the secret of creating abundance or affluence.

Spiritual master replied, "There are two goddesses, one is the goddess of knowledge and her name is Sarasvati. Pursue her love and give her your full attention. The other goddess is Lakshmi, she is the goddess of wealth, but when you pay more attention to Sarasvati then Lakshmi will become jealous and pay more attention to you, the more you seek the goddess of knowledge, the more the goddess of wealth will seek you. She will follow you wherever you go and never leave you, and the wealth you desire will be yours."

We were created capable of using our focused thought to draw unlimited abundance into our lives. Health, wealth, whatever our goals are, they are within our reach. It is important for us to set these goals, to give our attention to and draw to ourselves. Saying affirmations and prayers about your goals, visualizing with a clear mental pictures about your goals will bring them into reality. This is a method of focusing our attention.

*(unknown source)

Facing My Fears:

The Bumble Bee and Me

As a child, I had an encounter not with an E.T. but with this large black and yellow bumble bee. When you are five years old, they look really really big! This bumble bee must have decided that I looked juicy, because he started out for me. Upon seeing this action, I reacted. Only I got into the house behind the screen door before he did. But that did not really satisfy this bumble bee. He kept on trying to run into the screen to get me.

Wow, this encounter set up fears of being stung by any insect, but especially the fear of bumble bees. Years later, I took my children to a pond where they could swim, and as I sat on this sandy bank, I felt this sharp prick on my little toe. Immediately I felt this rippling of energy as I saw my foot starting to swell. I actually didn't panic. I stepped into the cool water thinking this would solve the situation. Well I tried. Soon I realized this wasn't going to help, I got the children loaded up in the car and home we went.' I had my foot into ice cubes and ammonia as soon as we got into the house. I called the doctor and he said, "Well, if you were going to die, it would already be too late, so I'll prescribe something that will help". Much to my dismay, the whole leg swelled up and I spent a week in bed.

About ten years later, after I had been introduced to a spiritual pathway, and to Reiki I, I had another encounter with a stinging creature. Walking up to the front door of my home, I heard this buzzing. Something was trapped in my hair. Unconsciously, I put my hand up to brush away the insect, only to realize, I was just stung. It was not a bumble bee. It was a WASP! My first thoughts were, "I had better get to the hospital." Too late! My son was already pulling out of the drive on a business call. Well, I calmed myself down immediately, went into the house, got out an ice cube, wrapped my wrist in a towel, sat down quietly and went into meditation. Soon I sensed it was time to look at my wrist, there was no swelling. In fact, there was no sign that anything had happened. What a blessing! It gave me encouragement that this spiritual outlook on life and Reiki really worked. The following day, only a red dot was on my wrist, showing me that it had really happened. I had stilled my heart, my fears, my anxiousness; and into God's grace I went. It worked! And why not? I believed it would.

Three Fingers and a Door

A story told to me over dinner one night, was about a lovely lady (Kay) who's Angel story appears elsewhere in this manual. On a trip to Mexico with a group of people, getting out of the car she put her hand up to grasp the support between the front and back windows. Someone slammed the door on three of her fingers. Quietly, but with urgency she said, "Someone please open the door, now". When they opened the door they found that her three fingers were flattened. Everyone started to get excited and she said, "Hush". She quietly went into meditation and put her other hand on the fingers to send the Reiki healing. After a few minutes, she removed her hand and the fingers were all back to normal, no bruising, no cuts, all okay. Not allowing the others' fears, she had gone into the stillness, and remembered Jesus the Master saying, "Ask and you shall receive", and she believed it".

Jeanne

The Healing of Bio-Programs

As has been discussed, all illness, disease and most accidents result from "incorrect" subconscious and supraliminal consciousness programing. These "incorrect" programs cause the energy of the mind/emotions to manifest blockages and imbalances in the physical body Because the cause of the dis-ease has not been addressed, the healing of the body will need to be repeated and repeated until the *root cause* of the dis-ease is brought into consciousness and corrected by "Divine" intervention.

While experiencing the bio-program-gram healing I learned that during early childhood, frequently by the age of seven, we develop our nine basic programs of humanity. These programs then direct the further development of the body and personality.

Human effort, knowledge and spirit alone cannot correct these programs without "Divine" healing assistance. Evidence to support this truth is seen daily by the numbers of people who stay in "therapy" and "self-help" programs year after year. Yes, they improve with sincere intention and hard work, but they <u>are</u> <u>not</u> <u>cured</u>.

My first experience with bio-program healing came at a time when I felt that all of the traditional support systems of the old world had let me down. Actually, I wasn't sure that I had not let them down! I was divorced, had lost my job, and my beloved father was not only dying, but in great pain daily.

I was exhausted, frightened and depressed when a friend suggested I contact "The Family Ark", a group administering and teaching bio-program healing. (see Bibliography section) Knowing that I had to find another way, I made the appointment without knowing anything about this process, because it *felt right.*

The group leader taught me to create my own visualization to address the program which "Divine guidance" had indicated needed healing first, I felt the weight of my problems lift. As my awareness was expanded, I experienced an indescribable sense of euphoria. I physically felt my spine realign, my heart muscles strengthen and my lungs clear. When I opened my eyes I realized that everything appeared sharper and clearer. A subsequent eye exam confirmed that I no longer required glasses for near-sightedness and astigmatism. As I stood I realized that internal organs in my abdomen had shifted and my entire body felt twenty pounds lighter; all in about half an hour!

I left my first session aware of the enormous amount of healing energy with which my body had been charged. Having always had fairly reliable ESP, I now found that faculty expanded to more than reading people; it was now enhanced with scents, sounds, and time/event currents.

The group leader advised me that I would probably sleep more as my body healed, and I continued my visualizations daily. I also journaled examples of daily occurrences which exemplified how healing and expanding now allowed me to be aware of things that my old program had blocked. Obviously, this old program had been a major block for me, preventing me from seeing alternatives and creatively solving problems.

While each program that was healed fostered wholeness and allowed the creation of functionally, joyful new programs for living, the next strongest impact came while healing my "Nurture" program. I truly wish there was a way to share - instantly, right this minute - with everyone, the unmeasurable joy and love I was filled with when all the emotional pain from the times I had felt unloved, rejected, or inadequate simply left with the realization that the actions of others had not "hurt" me. It was my inability to forgive that had caused my pain.

This release is true peace. To be at peace with yourself because you can love (nurture) yourself; to be at peace with others lovingly; to be at peace with animals, plants - - the very earth itself, as you extend and receive love - this is the gift and the blessing of the Divine. May you all follow the path which leads you there.

Healing of the basic programs of individuals is a new gift to humankind, carried out by a power beyond our own. As we progress in our evolution, we become aware of the need for this work and of the global quickening which has allowed us to open to the correction of our 3-D (three dimensional) human programing. The following is a list of Programs (not everyone requires healing of every program) providing an overview:

1) **Response to Quickening** - Reverses the powerful old world programs of boredom, lack of motivation, seeping away of life force, and death.

2) **Service to Reality** - Initial programing of one's relationship to the fact of living; i.e., signaling need and exploring daily reality. Healing of this program enables realization of and development with new design and situation.

3) **Utilization of Nurture** - Receiving answers to needs in the way answering is needed (love, support, abandonment issues).

4) **Utilization of Opportunities** - When this program is defective or blocked it can mask or misinterpret opportunity to such an extent that it is literally impossible for the person to recognize opportunity.

5) **Development** - The program for correct development of life form of the physical body.

6) **Expansion** - Expands awareness and enables expansion of identity.

7) **Mastering Zenithing** - Putting a purpose, value, idea, action or purpose at the top of one's energy focus, lifting the person toward what is zenithed.

8) **Hastening Gains** - Empowering what works and keeps on working.

9) **Collaborating to Foster Goodness** - Acting on one's own truth correctly in a context harmonizing with others' truth and the truth of the new world.

The results of mind/body bio-programing do not stop; eventually - auric healing occurs. When a critical mass of humanity has reached this "healed" state, we will enter a new world where there is *no yearning without an answer.*

iAsa

GUARDIAN ANGEL MEDITATION

Sit or lie down in a comfortable position. - Relax
Breathe the energy from top of your head, down through your body, and out the bottom of our feet into the roots of Mother Earth
Breathe in deeply, exhale through the mouth slowly
Relax and repeat, three times

Visualize yourself in a golden and white meadow, where wild flowers are all a bloom, the sun in streaming down, warm but not hot. And as you walk across this meadow towards the woods you are following the pathway that has been there for a long time.

As you reach the wood, you feel the coolness, the Serenity, the quietness. You continue following the pathway, walking slowly amongst the trees. Moss is growing along the path. Large boulders seem to be here and there with ferns and ivy growing up the tree bark.
Soon the pathway comes into a clearing, where there is a small waterfall, flowing down into a pond, the water is crystal clear. It looks like and it is a wading pool. We decide to step into this shallow water near the waterfall, and soon a slight breeze carries the spray of water misting over your body. It feels so clean, so pure.—letting go of any heavy burden or problems you may have, any negative attitudes, letting go and letting God be all there is. This beautiful energized water clearing and healing all the trappings we may have, angriness, tiredness, doubts, fears, hurts, we feel so light like a feather floating in the breeze; feeling lighter and lighter as we let go of responsibilities that are not ours.

As we gaze across the pond, we see an angel coming to us with a white rose with pink feathered edges. And this angel is placing this perfect rose into our hearts - reminding us we are perfect beings and one with our Divine source. The angel reminds us we are forever connected to this Divine Source, that we are angels that came to the earth vibration for the experience: that our guardian angels are the other half - keeping us safe, and as we allow our awareness of our guardian angel to grow, knowledge is available to us.

This perfect rose is vibrating and glowing within us. The energy is so immense I wonder how we can ever stay on earth when this feels so magnificent. We make a vow to hold this energy with us always throughout our daily lives - remembering, remembering.

This energy from the water that sprayed us: this energy from the rose within our hearts, flows throughout our bodies, into the roots of our feet, into Mother Earth's depths, down into the inner - world, grounding us, purifying us.

Our guardian angel places around us a cloak of intense white/silver/gold mesh cloth like angel wings wrapped around us, protecting us always. Our angel takes our hand and helps us from the pond of water, guides us to the bank where we see flowers and crystals, berries, and hear the birds singing. Our guardian angel whispers the name vibration into our ears.
As the name echoes in our ears, we know we have just been prepared for the Reiki initiation: ready to receive the symbols that will help us to always feel this energy, that Divine Source is working within us on our personal journey our bodies have been prepared, minds have been prepared, and our guardian angel will be there with us always.

Slowly now, start walking down the pathway through the woods, out into the sunshine, and across the meadow. The pathway is clear, the sun is gentle, the wild flowers smell heavenly.

Slowly come back into yourself.
Take a deep breathe, and exhale.
Return slowly to this reality.
Become aware that you are safe, here and grounded.

HAND POSITIONS - FRONT OF BODY

Directions: Wash hands from your elbows down before you begin doing healing work and after you finish the healing work. Release all: negativity, misqualified energies, and/or turmoil within. Sense your connection to your spiritual guides. You are the channel. The Reiki energy will be directed to where it is needed. Trust.

With the client lying on his back:

Position 1.
Head - with the base of your hands together, place them on the crown chakra (top of head) with your fingers facing toward the feet

Position 2.
Eyes - hands cupped together, thumbs touching, gently place your hands over the eyes with the fingertips resting on the cheeks - fingers pointing toward the feet

Position 3.
Ears - hands cupped, place individually over ears with fingertips pointing toward the feet

Position 4.
Base of Skull - slowing turn head to side and place one hand under the base of skull, then gently roll head to side to place other hand under the base of skull - both hands touching pointing towards the feet.

Position 5.
Shoulders - place hands on top of the shoulders with the fingertips over clavicle and pointing towards the feet

Position 6.
Throat / Thymus area - left hand under neck, right hand on throat / thymus area

Position 7.
Heart -   T-position or hands side by side over heart area (T-position recommended when working on the female gender)

Position 8.
Abdomen - (8a, 8b, 8c) place hands side by side moving across mid-section of the body, starting below the breasts to the hip area (major emotions held in this area)

Position 9.
Knees - do one knee at a time, one hand on top, one hand underneath (legs are going forward in life - this will be holding energy and will need clearing)

From the hip area down: ruffle and pull energy down legs (about three times) before going to feet for grounding and closing

Position 10.
Feet - (10a, 10b) place hands on feet for grounding

* Closing: gently ruffle down the whole body starting at head and working towards feet, close with infinity symbol or alternate method *see section Preparation for Giving a Reiki Treatment

Front of Body / Emotional area - When working with the front of the body, this is the emotion part of the physical body. A highly concentrated form of energy consciousness which stimulates a pattern of organic responses in the body. Can be felt physically and experienced mentally. Emotion is the fundamental manifestation of the vital life force, it cannot be seen or touched; but felt in a powerful form.

Center in divine source: emotional feelings or moods affect the body

See Below: Alternate method of Hand Positions:

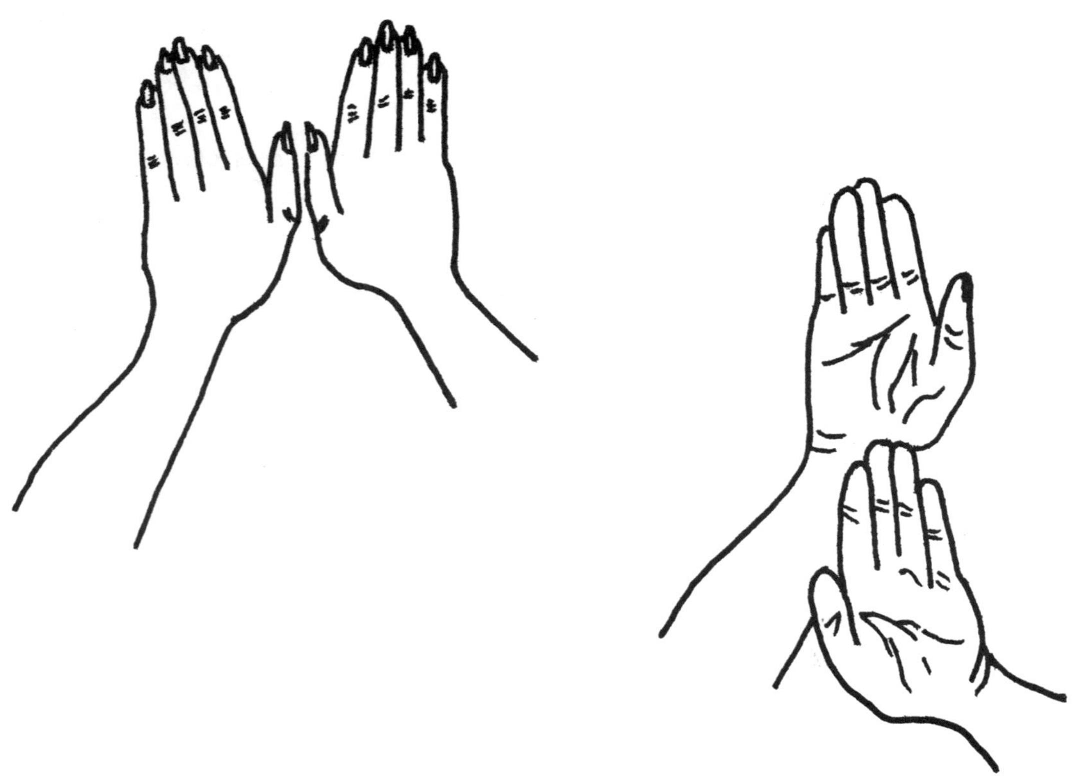

Below is a generic <u>frontal</u> view of the vital body organs:

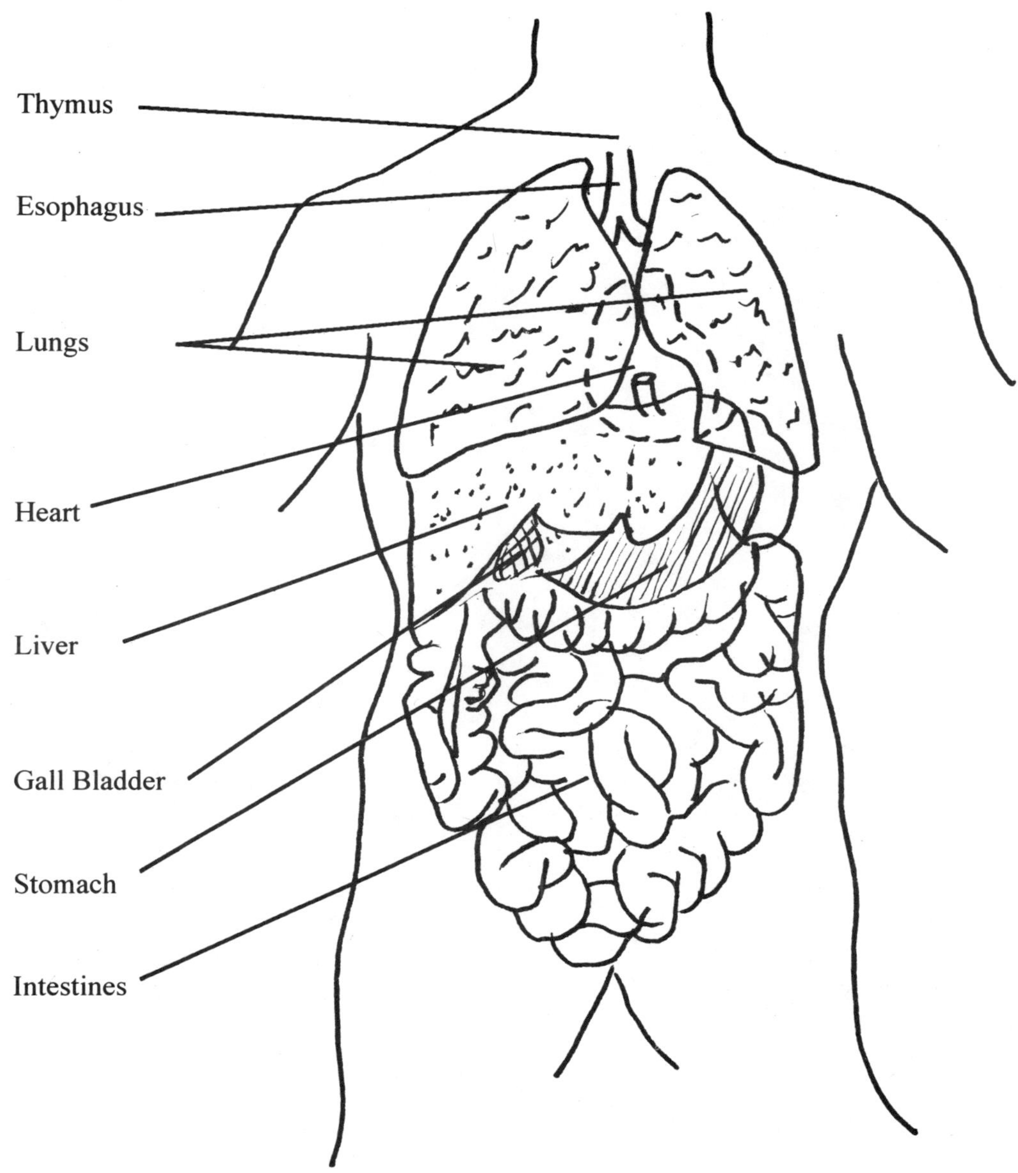

HAND POSITIONS - Front of Body

Directions: wash hands to elbows, release tensions and negativity, center yourself and sense your connection. Trust.

With the client lying on his back:

Position #1 - HEAD
(With the base of your hands together, place them on the top of head (crown chakra) with your fingers pointing towards the feet)

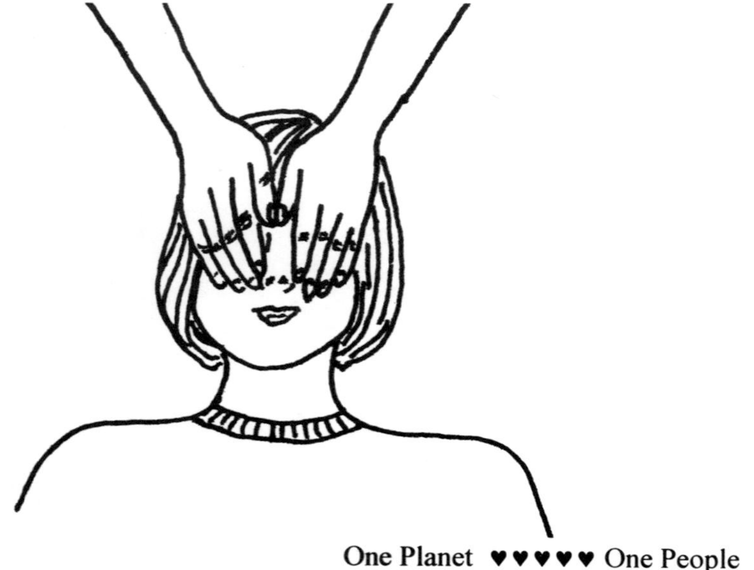

Position #2 - Eyes
(hands cupped together, thumbs touching, gently place your hands over the eyes with the fingertips resting on the cheeks - fingers pointing toward the feet)

Position #3 - Ears
(hands cupped, place individually over ears with fingertips pointing towards the feet)

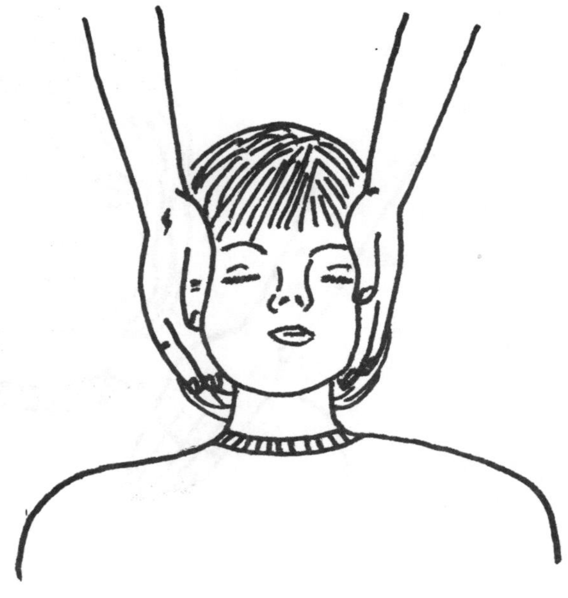

Position #4 - Base of Skull
(slowly turning head to the side, place one hand under the base of skull, then gently roll head to side to place other hand under the base of skull - both hands touching pointing towards the feet)

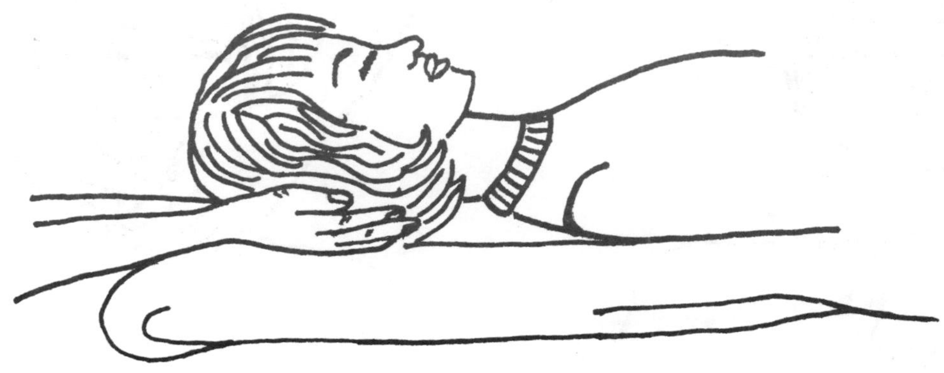

Position #5 - Shoulders
(place hands on top of the shoulders/ with the fingertips over clavicle and pointing towards the feet)

Position #6 - Throat / Thymus
(left hand under neck, right hand on throat / thymus area) see diagram of vital organs

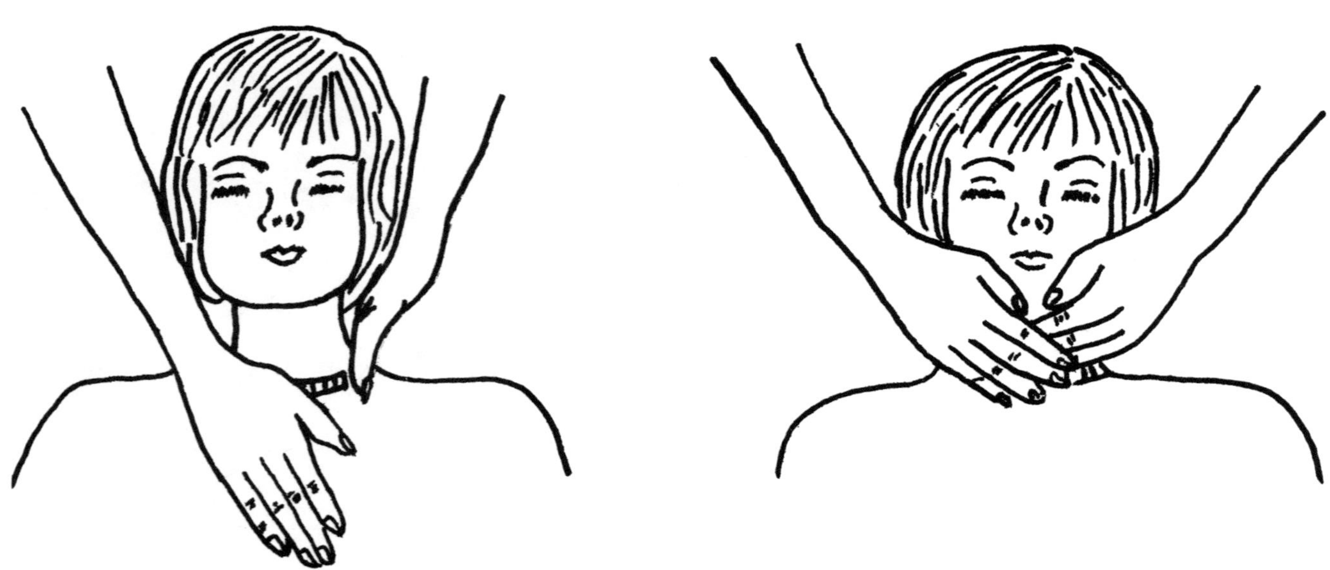

Position #7 - Heart
(T-position or hands side by side over heart area) T-position recommended when working on female gender

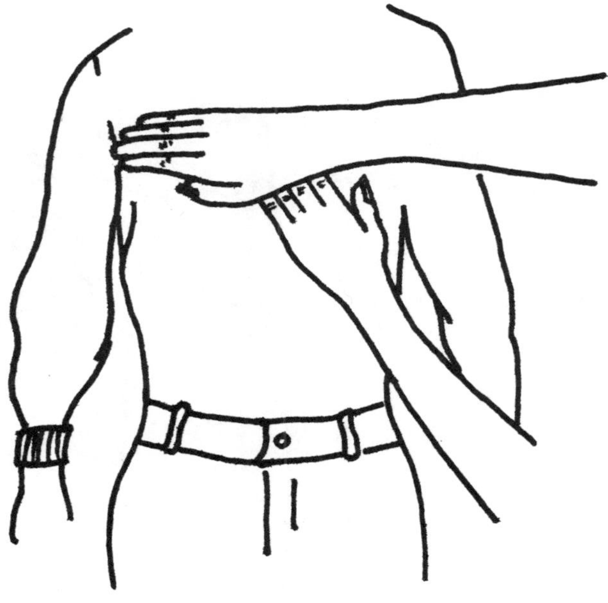

Position #8a - Upper Abdomen
(place hands side by side moving across mid-section of the body, starting below the breast area and working downward to hip area)

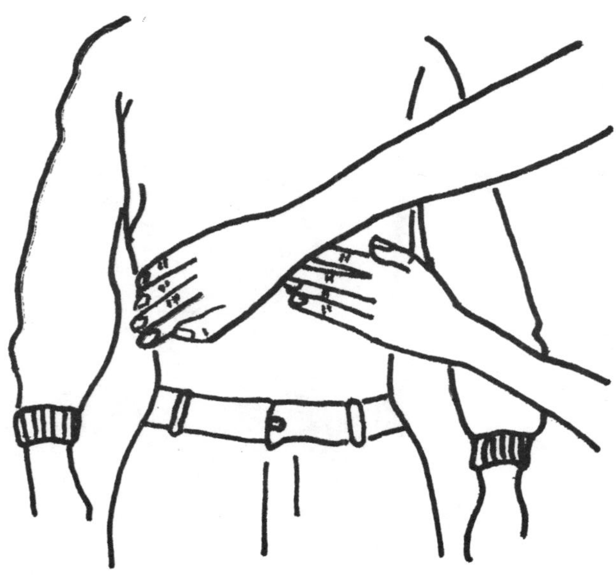

Position #8b - Middle Abdomen
(place hands side by side or alternate method moving across mid-section of the body, working downward to hip area)

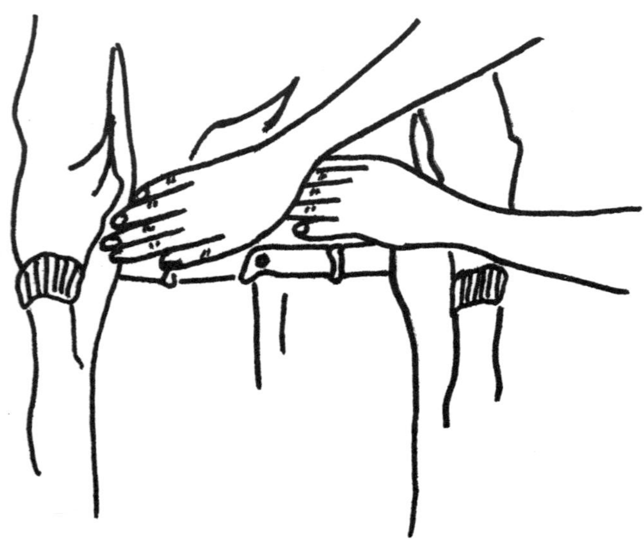

Position #8c - Lower Abdomen
(place hands side by side or alternate method working across lower abdomen to hip area)

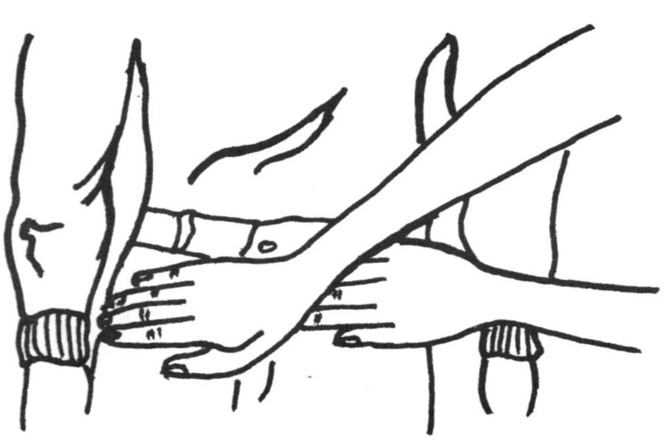

Position #9 - Knees
(do one knee at a time, one hand on top and on hand underneath) from the hip area down : ruffle
and pull energy down the legs - about three times before going to feet

Position #10 - Feet
(place hands at the bottom of feet for grounding)

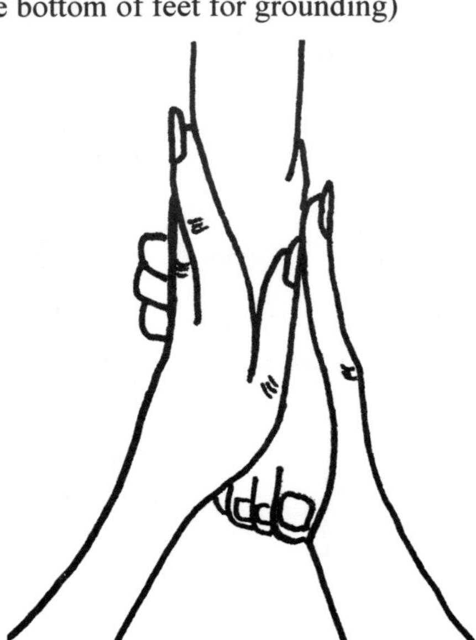

Closure: Gently ruffle the body three times and close with infinity symbol or alternate method.

Below is a generic <u>back</u> view of the vital body organs:

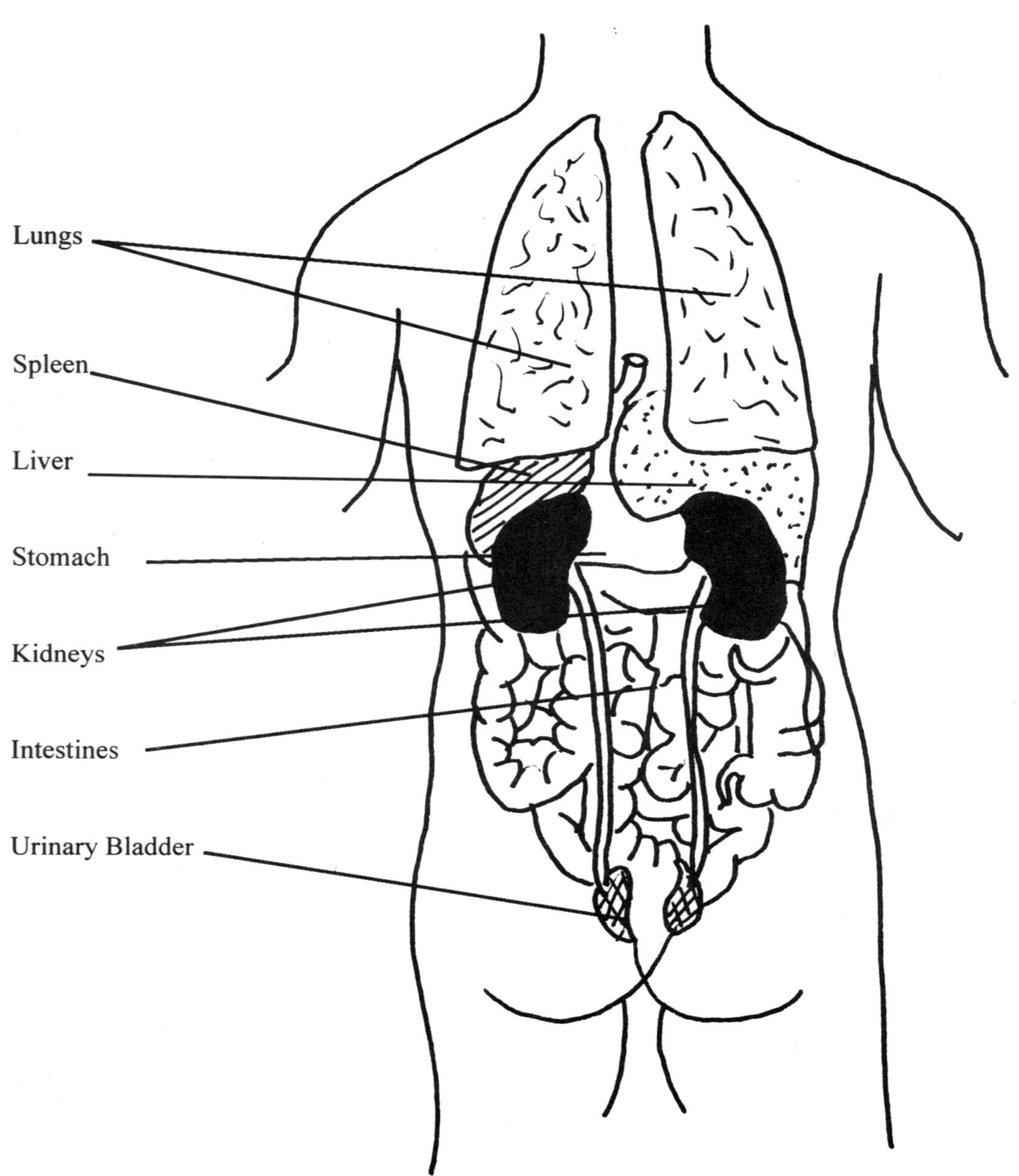

HAND POSITIONS - BACK OF BODY

With client lying on his stomach:

Position 11.
Top of Shoulders - standing looking towards feet - place hands on top of shoulders, fingertips towards feet

Position 12.
Back: Upper/Middle/Lower - position hands side by side (or alternate style) moving across the body, from upper back area to hip area

Position 13.
Leg Area - place hands on back of knees, pulling the energy down (i.e. position #9 - front of legs)

Position 14.
Feet - place hands on feet for grounding

* Closure: gently ruffle energy down the body from head to feet, three times, then use infinity symbol or alternate method to weave body energy together

Back of Body / Physical - when working with the back of the body, this is the physical will. This is mind governing principle that activates the atoms into manifestations of all degrees in the Universe. The essential attribute of the mind acts as a lever on matter and the consciousness makes the action occur. This in turn affects the aspects of the body energy fields and chakra system. Again the differences in these energy wheels depends upon the clients thoughts and will that interact with that part of the body.

Example: the body organs supplied by the chakra (energy wheel) will not get what is needed or will get too much focused energy - depending upon what the mind is focused on. If a lack or stress continues over a long period of time, this will start interacting with the other chakras (energy wheels) and their body organs and functions. Ultimately this will start the dis-easement and breakdown of the immune systems.

Self-Attunement: one hand over top of head (crown chakra) and the other hand moving downward over the other chakras (*wheels of energy) * see diagram of energy systems

Self-Balance: one hand on top of head (crown chakra) and the other hand on lower back, then reverse positions.

HAND POSITIONS - Back of Body

With the client lying on his stomach:

Position #11 - Top of Shoulders
(standing looking at the feet - place hands on tops of shoulders, fingertips towards the feet)

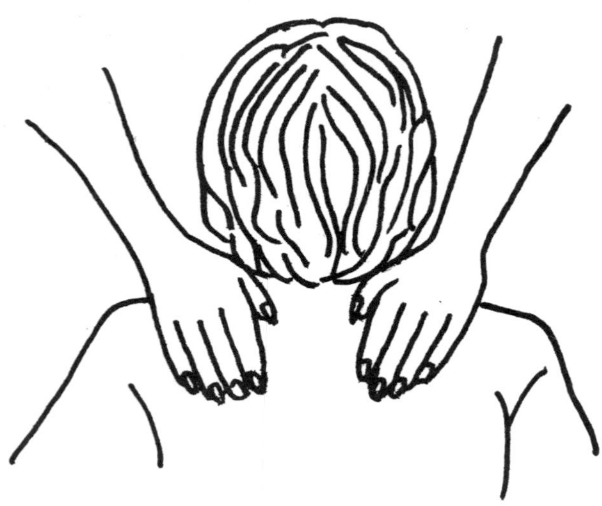

Position #12a - Back: Upper
(position hands side by side or alternate method moving across the body, from the upper back to the hip area)

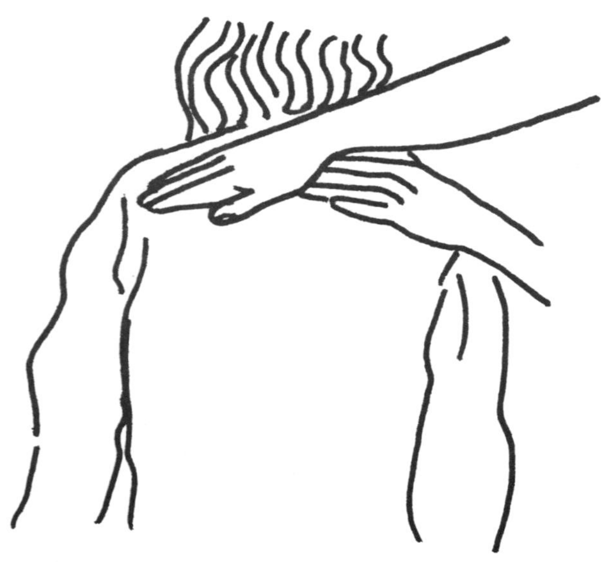

Position #12b - Back: Middle
(position hands side by side or alternate method moving across the body, from the middle back to the hip area)

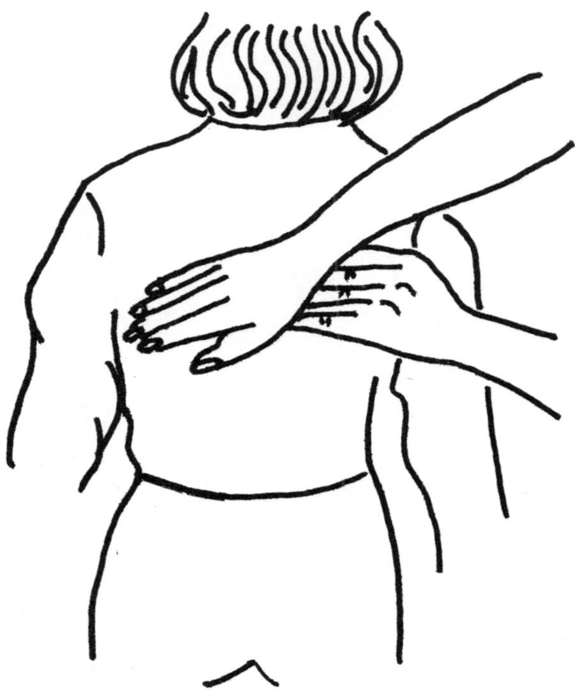

Position #12c - Back: Lower
(position hand side by side or alternate method moving across body ending around the hip area)

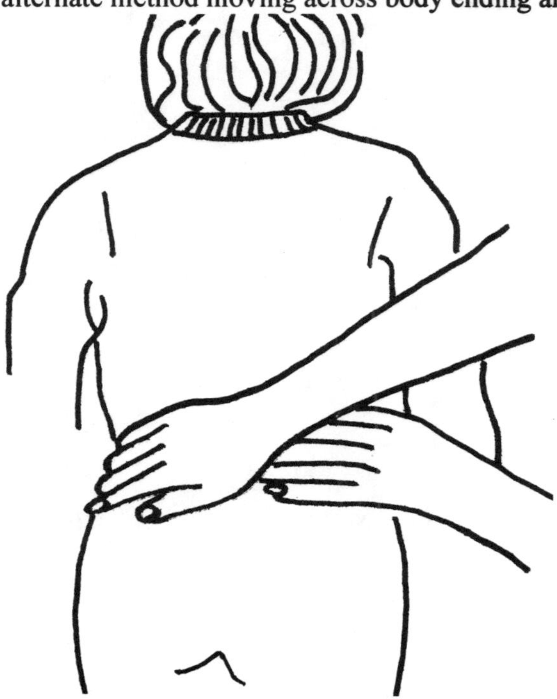

Position #13 - Legs
(place hands on back of knees, pulling the energy down the legs)

Position #14 - Feet
(place hands on feet for grounding)

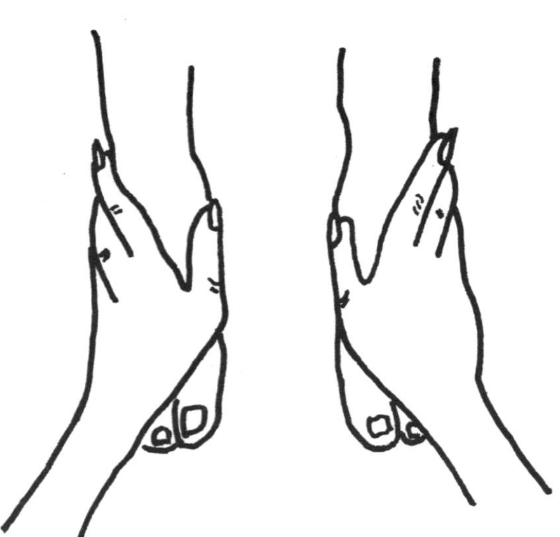

* Closure: Gently ruffle down the energy down the body three time and close with infinity symbol or alternate method. *see Preparation for Reiki Treatment

BODY MIND WORK - FACILITATION METHOD

Energy is energy is energy, consistently ever-changing within natural patterns.

As your spiritual self is open and energy fills you, the creative source flows, allowing connectedness (oneness with your client) and thus a knowingness of what energy needs facilitation (movement), <u>where</u> and <u>how.</u>

Guidelines may be given and logic is a foundation: but, do not allow the logic to interfere with creativeness, the essence of healing, joyfulness and love.

<u>SESSION</u>

Center Self:

°　　　connection - state mentally or verbally your intention, this creates a focus of the unconditional　love frequency (vibration) that always surrounds us (like water to fish in the ocean)

Opening Stretch
(individual facilitator)

°　　　place fingertips along the occipital ridge (base at back of head) and provide slight traction, place hands on sacral reflex at ankles, while cupping heels and provide slight traction

(team facilitation)

°　　　one person provides the <u>head</u> hold
　　　one person provides the <u>ankle</u> hold
　　　both provide traction simultaneously

Scanning System

The human system is an energy imprint (grid or blueprint) which manifests in physical form (the body). Determine areas requiring balance with an evaluative energy scan. Particularly note knees and ankles.

Interventions

Intervention techniques are used to balance energy as required through the clients system - within the body and beyond. * see diagrams on energy field - Section: Energy and Chakras

°　　　Knees - check that energy flows through this area and is not "leaking out" (when leaking, seal with hand "sandwich method" (medially-laterally or anteriorly-posteriorly)

°　　　Ankles - assure energy flows through ankles and out the soles of the feet

Removal of Crystallized Energy

- (left hand) hold energy of the area
- (right hand) lazers with fingertips, heats or melts with hand chakra
- can also lazer with third eye
- lazering is often a spiraling motion - sometimes a "cross-fire"
  when complete pluck out and discard misqualified or negative energies to **all consuming violet flame*** (neutralizing)   *(St. Germaine of Ascended Masters)
- fill and seal with (left hand) boosted by (right hand) during this process
  instruct the client with self intention, visualization, color, sound, etc.

Placement of Energy Grids

Balance Area
- insert via visualization, intention (i.e. time-release capsule or pyramid for pain relief)
- seal when complete

Sandwich
- place hands opposite - each with body between
  (i.e. one hand on top of body, one hand on bottom body in direct correlation)
- focus on energizing area

Cross-Fire
- use index and middle fingers of both hands to cross-fire small areas

Connect any chakra point with any area requiring balance.

Torso Energy Moving Contacts

- (right hand) with middle finger connecting tip of tailbone - (stronger pressure)
- (left hand) on any blocked point above (right hand position) draw out contact

- (left hand) index finger on third eye
- (right hand) on any blocked point of body - strongest projecting into contact

- any point connected with solar plexus - keeping (left hand) higher than (right hand)
  strongest balancing contact

Flowing Figure (Infinity) Sacral-Cranial Balance

sandwiching (posterior and anterior) - start at sacrum/pubic area and balance
alternate bottom hand to top (and vise versa) to next hand width - up the spine
continue process up the body through the third eye area

Emotional Release from Life Times

º   (left hand) over heart
º   (right hand) over navel - (solar plexus and sacral chakra area)

Emersion

º   visualize holding a vessel above the client or surrounding the client (i.e. cocoon) and allow the energy to pour upon and /or to envelop the client

Intention During Session

º   focus use of energy via: hands, fingers, third eye, visualize with the mind
º   invoke presence of energy imprints of anything needed
         (i.e. sound, color, crystals, water flowing, plants, herbs, essences)
º   invoke assistance from angels, fairies, Jesus, Buddha, ascended masters, power animals

Ending Session

º   when in balance, aura brush to clear energy field, seal with infinity sweep, ground at feet

Give Thanks - Detach

Client self-empowerment is promoted via active participation in their process. This exponential energy, thus quickens and intensifies results. Use your voice to facilitate journeys, places of past/future lives, any messages.

Encourage participation via:
(education, music, movement, progressive relaxation, breath work, toning, visualization)

Go with loving tenderness for yourself, for serving of humanity is a most reverent calling, which first requires self nurturing.

Joan Essig

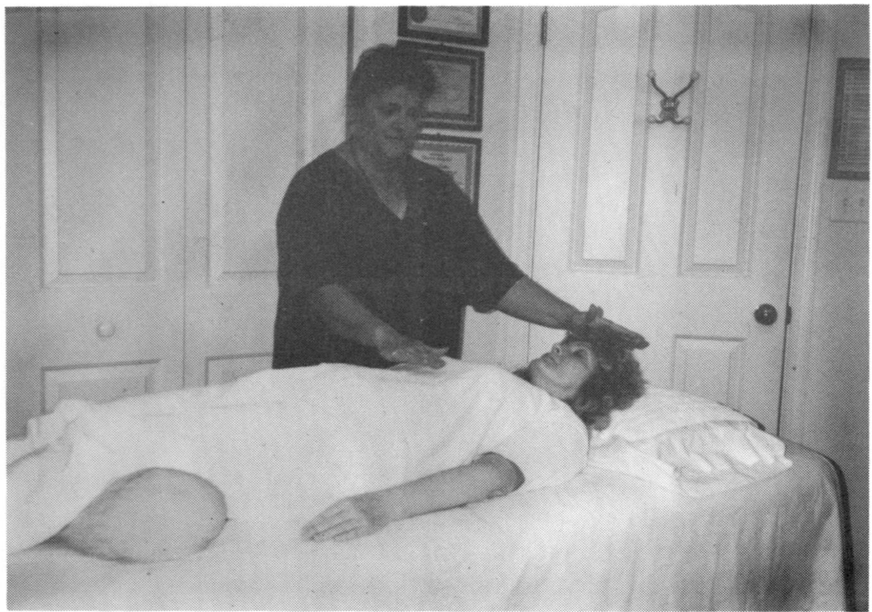

Three Point Treatment:

When visiting someone in the hospital, or if there is a small amount of time and space in which to help someone that is in need, the following example would be beneficial:

1) Place one hand on top of head (crown chakra) - area where miracles work - mind center

2) Place the other hand on the navel area (solar plexus/sacral area) -
     the power or personal issue center

3) When finished, ground by touching the feet and holding briefly -
     sense your connection has been made

4) Close up

This technique can be used with the client either lying on his back or his stomach or even in a chair. You can either physically touch or hold your hands 2-4 inches from the body. Have the client visualize peace, and moving the energy (the atoms) through out the body from the head to the feet and out. Have the client address the area in his own body that is feeling distressed, which will activate the healing in a shorter amount of time.

Reiki "Team" Facilitated Treatment

Reiki today is coming to a New Age of use. There is no wrong way to use Reiki when the intention is for the best interest and highest good of the client.

Reiki helps unite people in a cause for greater consciousness and well being. Reiki is not just for the chronically ill client. Though Reiki does work if given time, however we are a society that wants immediate results. Reiki is also for maintenance of well being. Healing is a daily process, as ongoing as cellular replenishment.

We have been devoting time for the past several years in what we call "Team" or "Group" work. Referred to as "Reiki Open House" or "Reiki Clinic". We have enjoyed working on each other for maintenance, but we also have given mini-treatments for those that are new to Reiki or in need of a Reiki healing. Several of us get together with one objective in mind, that of making another individual feel better. It's a time of laughter, sharing and caring.

When we have three people, we use the Three Point Treatment:
One at the head (crown), one at navel area (solar plexus/sacral), one at feet. We have learned to speak non-verbally and have learned when to move on in the work. When there are only two people: One starts at the crown area, and one at the navel area/mid-section; both gradually work down the body.

Our team work has evolved in different aspects. Where some individuals may have a strong leaning towards working with crystals, and others toward Native American belief systems (i.e. feathers, crystals, herbs, rattle); other examples are those in tune with the angelic kingdom, healing pulses (vibrational), toning (sound), and the ascended masters (channeling messages) all healing using the universal life force energy.

Our work goes along with some of the ancient rituals and customs that seem to have incorporated aspects of Reiki into their ceremonies. When Native American Medicine Men performed a healing, they were working for the good of the whole as well as that of the individual. The Medicine Man may not have been using the exact methods that are used in Reiki, but the format and results were the same. Some healings were done with several people participating, lending their thoughts and visions to the healing work with the central conductor being the Medicine Man. The helpers would often wear masks, had feathers for smudging and other tools for specific healing purposes. The Medicine Man would often perform his healing with a rattle (vibrational) or feather (ruffling) or both. The group focused on healing the individual in need. They were indeed working for one planet ♥ one people.

We have even changed our attitude about traditional handshakes - moving into a new dimension, we sense the touching of spirit and not just a social greeting.

Our special <u>Reiki Hugs</u> are in another section of this manual. No slap happy hugs for us!!

Reiki Team

One Planet ♥ ♥ ♥ ♥ ♥ One People

Client Status Form
Health Questionnaire and Release Form

I am requesting Reiki services on my own initiative and realize the Reiki practitioner does not prescribe substances, diagnose ailments or practice medicine. It is recommended that I see a licensed health care professional, a licensed physician, or licensed psychologist along with any alternative health care treatments I am endorsing.

A Reiki Session is given for the following purposes: (stress reduction, balancing of chakras, before and after surgery, pre-natal conditions, mental and emotional abusive situations, relaxation).

Date: _________________________   Signature:_______________________________

Name ____

Address ____ .

City/State/Zip____

Telephone No. _______________________________________

Physical Remarks:

____

Session Date	Fee	Reiki Session Treatment Remarks

REIKI TREATMENT GUIDE

IMPORTANT: Always begin the treatment with a complete basic treatment, working each place until the need is met, then go to the affected part that is outside the basic treatment area. When taking prescribed medications, please sure to consult your doctor along with your Reiki alternate method of healing.

SPECIFIC TREATMENTS FOR THE HEAD:

Sinuses, Post-Nasal Drip:
Basic treatment for the head

Earache, Draining, Hearing:
Basic treatment of the head

High Blood Pressure:
Treat the hard and brittle glands on the side of the neck - helps heart also

Voice:
Treat the larynx, using the whole hand

Mouth:
Toothache, (cavity): first - treat the cheek and jaw of the child, gives relief
Adult - treatment relieves pain temporarily

Canker Sores, Coated Tongue, Cancer of the Mouth:
Treat the bottom of the feet

Headache:
From a cold - basic treatment to head, throat and bronchi

Migraine:
Basic front treatment, especially ovaries & uterus/prostate, then treat the head, thyroid, liver and endocrine system

Goiter:
Give complete treatment, throat, ovaries/prostate - this is not acute
Palpitations may be a symptom of endocrine imbalance

SPECIFIC TREATMENTS FOR THE FRONT:

Colds, Fever, Heart:
Treat above the diaphragm to the heart area

Diabetes:
Treat pancreas. Client must adhere to diet, blood tests, and take only needed amount of insulin, when client's insulin need declines to 3 units, consult your doctor - continue treatments until stabilized

Ulcers, Stomach acid, Cancer:
Make stomach alkaline, no fried greasy or harsh food (Takata's recipes are available)

Gall Bladder, Nausea, Balance:
Treat above and behind the ears - gallstones can be removed by constant treatment, from **reaction to** climax may be 4-6 consecutive treatments, then taper off to 3 times a week

Heart Condition:
Basic treatment to the front, then the heart. - Do <u>not turn</u> the client

Pleurisy:
You can turn the patient back over to treat the lung area

Pneumonia:
Treat front - treat entire lung area putting hands under the back, until crisis is over or temperature breaks - give as much warm lemonade or ascorbic acid as possible, client sweats - gently towel toward the heart to remove sweat, Do NOT put client on stomach with pneumonia

Childbirth:
Frequent treatments all during pregnancy (3 times a week) helps for a painless childbirth - treat abdominal area for mounting delivery pain, treat coccyx and rectal area for birth preparation

Cancer:
Complete treatment, then glands on the side of the body and back - treat affected area, do this daily for a month

Breast Lumps:
Complete treatment, female organs, ovaries, uterus, thyroid, lump, affected area, then breast
Results: toxins cleansed, organs revitalized - lump begins to dissolve

SPECIFIC TREATMENTS FOR THE BACK AND FEET:

Arthritis:
Complete treatment, abdomen, when organs are balanced and vitalized, change begins - kidney area
A change of diet is needed

Mental and Emotional Stress:
Treat head first, then solar plexus, front / left side of back (one hand front/one hand back)

Stomach Acid, Gall Bladder, Liver:
Treat solar plexus, right side of back

Backaches:
Basic treatment on back then down the spine, kidney area

Lower Back Pain:
Complete treatment, lower spine, prostate, rectum

Hemorrhoids:
Lower back, prostate, rectum

Epilepsy:(An electrical storm in the brain)
Give complete treatment, head, front and back DAILY for one month - with improvement taper off
gradually to one treatment per week, until well - healing takes six months to a year

Babies:
Treat the bottom of the feet, a sharp cry means stomach pain - treat 20/40 minutes

Leukemia:
Complete treatment, then spleen

Sties:
Complete treatment, liver, kidneys to release built up toxins

Note: Credit is given to Hawaya Takata's lineage - Reiki Masters and Students

REIKI MEDITATION IN A FOREST

Start:
Relax in a comfortable position.
Take a long, slow, deep breath.
Exhale slowly through the mouth.
Relax and repeat three times.

Envision yourself on a path in a dense, lush, green forest. The path is winding, deeper and deeper into the foliage. You are aware of the scent of honeysuckle and jasmine. The birds are singing.
A gentle breeze rustles the leaves on the trees and branches of the trees.
The sun filters down through the trees in beautiful patterns of light.
You are coming to a small clearing.
The ground is cool and soft. You sit down, feeling totally relaxed.
You look up to the sky and see a small rainbow of colors that appear to be swirling above your head.
Watch this circle of colors. Allow yourself to experience this for a few minutes.

Now you see the circle of rainbow colors becoming a funnel of energy descending towards you.
You feel wonderful as the funnel of light travels down through your body.
In the center of the circle, you are the center of your self.
Trust your knowing. Trust your intuition.
The colors fill you, yet extend from you.
You feel at one with all the colors, the energy.
Trust this connection of energy within your heart and mind of knowing.
Allow yourself to totally "sense" this energy.

Take the time to receive that color from every sense. See it. Taste the flavor. Touch it. Listen for the sound of the color. Catch the fragrance of the color.
Take time to note the colors that you have chosen.

As you begin to "sense" the colors lifting up and away from you, release them, gently. See the pattern and circles as they leave your body,
Becoming a tighter pattern of circles as they go,
Blending, becoming the most beautiful color you've ever seen.
(You may see a new color that is forming.)

As you send this energy up and out into the universe, you sense a greater love and connection than ever before.
A connection of helping heal yourself, the forest, and the planet.
You have a sense of being whole, at peace, healed, energized.

The essence of the colors and the energies stay with you.
Experience it.

Become aware of your surroundings:
The clearing, the birds singing, the sweetness of the air.
Open your mind to the forest.
Take a deep breath, exhale.
You are completely in the "now" and grounded and balanced.

Lumis

REIKI HUGS

Having taken Reiki, even a simple **hug** has more influence over its purpose. As you give or receive a Reiki hug, you "feel" the person's energy that you are hugging. This exchange of energy is whole and pure. The person receiving the hug, if not familiar with Reiki may simply feel a sense of warmth or well-being, a peacefulness. For that space and time you have shared energy, replenishing, building and extending your own as well as that of the other person. It is like a mini-healing.

Begin noticing the way you hug. You will begin to notice the differences and look forward to a shared hug rather than a pat-a-pat on your back, which is disruptive and jarring. You will take pleasure in the greetings, knowing you have made a beautiful connection with another human being.

BLESSINGS

Esoteric meaning: a mass of energy psychically produced that is healing, soothing and pleasant to receive; decree the electrical impulses and direct to a certain designation; (i.e. to improve health, to bring about a good experience, to wish well).

Blessing Way: (Native American, Navaho) a special ceremony in which the whole tribe participates, raises the vibrations which can be used to heal and bring abundance to the tribe.

Blessed Water: Fill a dark blue glass or jar with water, either Reiki the water by sending energy or using the Reiki symbols with the intention of the water being blessed.

I have a friend who does this on a regular basis, her cats enjoy drinking the water daily and are exceptionally healthy. In fact, the cats won't drink any other water but this energized Reiki blessed water. Intention, and so it is!

SMUDGING

(Native American) to burn a special plant - usually sage or sweet grass in an area before a ceremony; (i.e. Medicine Wheel, Sweatlodge, Firewalk). Smudging is used before healing work, or other spiritual workshops.

Ritual: smoke from the sage or sweetgrass is fanned, usually with a feather, throughout the room or area from each of the four directions. The smudging cleanses the atmosphere of any misqualified energies that have gathered from thought forms in that area. Meditative music is also used along with doing this ritual. Smudging yourself before or after doing healing work is wonderful. It produces a feeling of freshness through out your own energy system.

CRYSTAL INFORMATION

The receptivity and search for knowledge about crystals has intensified in today's society. As we cross the threshold of the Golden Age of Knowing, the essence of crystals and stones has developed. Crystals have become tools for healing energy. Crystals are instruments of power to embrace, develop and manifest the light within. It is important that we do not lose the fact that "we are the light", and the crystals are guides or tools, a bond with Mother Earth.

Required: **when doing** a crystal healing

1) a clear mental focus when doing a crystal healing
2) letting go of any personal emotions or problems
3) art of giving - intention
4) amethyst will help your intuitiveness
5) being aware of the power of the crystals and body's electromagnetic fields

Experienced: **when receiving** a crystal healing

1) will bring more light force and color into auric field
2) opportunity to let go and let God take over
3) any mental or emotional blockages may surface to consciousness
4) as auric field becomes infused with light, a vibrational field rises
5) outdated belief systems can cause a revision of attitude, works with heart and mind centers

Environmental and Prayer for Protection:

Crystals are to be cleansed before and after a treatment by putting them outside in the sun or rain, using sage and smudging or washing with blessed water. (Native American) crystals can be put outside during the Full Moon and New Moon phases (a powerful time). If you are aware of a planetary energy grid, place the crystals there. If this is not available, putting the crystals on a window sill in the sun, or rinsing with sea salt water will work.

Clear yourself for work and repeat an affirmation (example below). Imagine the white light coming into the crown and flowing through you to the feet and roots and into Mother Earth (Native American). Seeing this light as clearing you, protecting you, grounding you, intensifying you and radiating out of your heart center for the preparation of the healing to begin.

I call upon the Light of the Great White Brotherhood
I call upon the God and Goddess Balancing Energies
I call upon the Light of the Great Central Sun
I call upon the Great White Buffalo Spirit
I call upon the Divine Light of own Beingness
I call upon the Endless Source of Light for Strength and Protection

One Planet ♥ ♥ ♥ ♥ ♥ One People

Clearing the room is necessary before and after each crystal healing session of any misqualified energies or psychic debris. An open window, smudging with sage or sweetgrass, lighting a candle is helpful; plus the use of Reiki symbols for empowerment and being in a positive frame of mind - intention. Music for meditation and the quieting of the mind, will also be helpful for releasing and clearing out.

The following is a guide of crystals used with the different chakras:

(A crystal ceremony and ritual will be performed at the conclusion of each Reiki Training Session)

Root Chakra:
(Root or base chakra concerns our connection with Mother Earth, our foundation, the Kundalini center, physical energy and the material reality)

Suggestions: Red Garnet
Jasper
Black Onyx
Black Obsidian
Smoky Quartz

Spleen/Sacral Chakra:
(Deals with emotions, intuition, friendliness, creativity; our self worth and confidence)

Suggestions: Tigers Eye
Carnelian
Jasper
Topaz
Amber
Citrine

Solar Plexus Chakra:
(Deals with center of personal power, natural skills, aptitudes, mental emotion; also associated with our center of intelligence)

Suggestions: Turquoise
Malachite
Azurite
Chrysocholla
Clear Quartz

Heart Chakra:
(Bridge between physical and spiritual; symbolizes the awakening of spirituality, center of our compassion, unconditional love, our most vulnerable wheel of light, connects with our immune system of thymus and Peyers Patches)

Suggestions:	Green Jade	Pink Tourmaline
	Adventurine	Rose Quartz
	Malachite	Emerald
	Rhodonite	Ruby

Throat Chakra:
(Deals with our center of communication, being able to express ourselves, spiritually open to clairvoyance)

Suggestions:	Lapis	Blue Sapphire
	Blue Lace Agate	Sodalite
	Peridot	Azurite
	Aquamarine	Celestite

Third Eye - Brow Chakra:
(Deals with the center of our intuition and psychic powers, ability to tune into our divine source, astral traveling, past lives, visionaries)

Suggestions:	Sugalite	Alexandrite
	Lapis	Clear Quartz
	Amethyst	Gem Silica
	Azurite	Fluorite (purple/white/blue)

Crown Chakra:
(When this center is fully opened, spirituality is omnipresent, you live in the light, the silver cord connects with our pineal and pituitary areas attaching our etheric body to our physical body and allows our astral traveling without disconnecting from our physical being)

Suggestions:	Clear Quartz (double terminator-pointing to aura and crown)	
	Fluorite	White Sapphire
	Lapis	Amethyst
	Diamond	

LAZER ACTION

Why Lazer Action???

Thought: All thought occurs in measureless space and is recorded in measurable electric (electro-magnetic) patterns, in what we call the cosmic universal consciousness. Within this space, this Thought (form), exists the results of Thought = Material or Matter.

Universe: The created universe is a record of a Thought or Thinking universe; and is made up of Thought Forms. Created universe is an electric record of all the universal consciousness or mass consciousness.

Thoughts created Matter - Matter forms a residue or a crystallization if the thought produced is:
1) fear thought, 2) repetitive thought, 3) deep rooted or (soul) thoughts

Fear Thoughts:
abusive incidents, incest, beatings, war, accidents, fears, ceaseless worry

Repetitive Thoughts:
divorce, legal battle, frustrations with work, financial, relationships

Deep Rooted Thoughts:
a) thoughts or ideas formed as a child in the subconscious, that are brought up as remembrances in our daily life; on a conscious level we are not aware of many of these thoughts
b) patterns developed by societal thinking, from family heritage, or passed on from one generation to the next
c) sexual, physical and mental abuse as a child

Our bodies are the material record of the thoughts which we have allowed to flow through it. We can erase, cancel, change or transfer these patterns of thought through the process of Reiki healing and/or with the lazer technique of Reiki. The material thought then returns to the universal consciousness, transmuted by the universal life force energy of light.

Using Reiki Lazer Technique:

1) is letting go and letting the God consciousness into all of the cells, atoms molecules with focused light beams of energy magnified

2) these ultra-frequencies (lazer) move at a different vibratory rate and work with the atoms and space, affecting the cells of the body

3) client helps identify the thought form crystallization and focuses on the release of this matter from a crystallization to light source

4) client recognizes his responsibility to change the negative thoughts into positive ones with affirmations, and to change the programming patterning (i.e. Louise Hay book - "You Can Heal Your Body")

STAR MAN

I see and feel his energy, I know him by the name of "Star Man'

I have been told he is from far away, from the Star Clan.

There is much celebration, awaiting for the final day

Thunder and dancing, and mask made of clay,

The memories are dim, but the celebrations have not gone astray,

We continue to dance, the dance of the Phoenix, and pray.

The drumming, the dance, the spirit journey to the stars

That is the way for us now, cause the journey is far.

But my Star Man comes here, its easier so he says,

My memories are dim, my way is unclear,

My "Star Man" will guide me and show me the way,

His energies are blue and white mists, his eyes are so bright

He looks like a Star, he'll show me the way, into the Light.

I know him by the name of "Star Man", he is from the Star Clan

The Thunder hides his star vehicle, but he is part of the plan.

Wind Dancer

BODY AWARENESS AND NUTRITION
by Dr. Stephanie Story

We may at times wish we did not have to be encumbered by this physical body that appears to limit us. In fact, without the body, we cannot do our soul's work.

If we neglect our bodies, we are limiting our receptivity to the influx of spirit, even though the effects of neglect may not be visible immediately. The limitation occurs in at least two ways:

1)   If not properly cared for, the body, directed by the vital force, must devote more of its attention to tasks related to basic survival, such as; maintaining biochemical equilibrium, repairing damage and protecting itself from exogenous as well as endogenous toxic influences.

2)   The process of expanded consciousness or spiritual awareness entails subtle changes in the molecular vibrational rate of each cell of the body. Under nourished cells or biochemical unbalanced tissues are limited in their vibratory rate and thus unable to receive or withstand the higher intensity vibrations that accompany the influx of Spirit. It is our receptivity to spiritual influences that allows us the avenue to co-create with Spirit, in so doing, serve humanity.

Not only must we ensure physical health in order to do this, but, to the degree of our commitment to working with Spirit, we must provide a vessel (the body) that is as finely tuned as possible.

Learning to live within the confines of a physical body and to care for it is, I believe, one of the major spiritual lessons of earthly existence. Learning to live with a body means respecting a sacred creation, part of what it means to respect all life, including our own. It means loving the body for the opportunity it gives us to carry out our work here - work that is unique to existence on earth and that cannot be done in any other plane. It means learning the limitations of the body and how to properly care for the body. It means knowing what is appropriate care and nourishment for the body at a given time. That may mean what kind of food does this body need now? What kind of rest? What kind of play? What kind of exercise, bodywork, counseling, spiritual practice, or what? And more than just knowing, it means respecting that knowing and it means loving yourself enough to take action and provide for that need.

A word must be said here regarding those who embrace the power of the mind and positive thinking so completely that they use this as rationalization for not attending to their needs. Instead they believe an affirmation or prayer will protect them from harmful influences, (food, air, water). I do not mean to minimize the power of prayer or affirmations, nor do I deny the power of the mind to transform physical substance.

I would only suggest that if such a belief is motivated from a place of wanting to avoid the responsibility or the learning that associated with for the physical, that person might be sorely disappointed in the eventual outcome. Sometimes this motivation is so deep that it is completely hidden from the conscious mind of the believer,

One of the essential ways we must learn to care for the body is through diet and nutrition. The old saying, "you are what you eat," is essentially true. The building blocks for replenishing the cells of our body, which are completely renewed every seven years, can only come from the substances we ingest or inhale. Without proper nutrition our cells do not have adequate or appropriate substances (amino acids, carbohydrates, fats, minerals, vitamins, enzymes, etc.) to use in carrying out their function or in building new cells and tissue. Biochemical imbalance at the cellular level is the distant procurer to dysfunction and eventual pathology. The body's tremendous compensating mechanisms can mask the foolishness of improper diet for years, but not without hidden costs that only later become apparent. It is much easier to prevent a "disease" than cure it.

Making Dietary Changes

When you are ready to make some positive dietary changes, it is natural to want some general rules to help guide you. Because of individual genetics and variable responses to environmental influences, it is very difficult to establish guidelines that will work for everyone. What is nutritious food for one may be harmful to another. Individual questioning must be encouraged. One's inner sense must provide guidance when general guidelines do not seem to work.

The first thing to realize is that the most important changes are those that you will continue to practice for the rest of your life. Experience shows that, while there are certainly exceptions, gradual changes, changes that can be incorporated into your daily life, are those that will continue to be practiced. While I always encourage as much change as anyone feels they want to make, please realize that if it seems like changes are too difficult to maintain, perhaps you are trying to do too much too fast. Fine. Just cut back on a few new things and keep on going. You have not failed, even if you have to revise your plan. Even one new, healthful habit or dropping one old, unhealthy habit is step in the right direction.

Some Simple Guidelines

1) Upgrade the quality of food you eat:
      (unprocessed food, because processed **depletes enzymes, vitamins and minerals,** chemicals added back for flavor)

2) Check out labels before buying:
      (avoid hydrogenated oils and fats, avoid **ingredients you cannot pronounce)**

3) Having a good water filter:
      (removal of chemicals, **chlorine, fluoride, and trihalomethanes, bacterial and protozoan contaminants)**

4) Air purifier:

      (one that generates ozone and negative **ions are most effective)**

5) Eating only natural whole pure foods:
      (vegetables, fruits, grains, nuts and seeds)

6) Fresh raw foods:
      (enzymes aids in digestion, helps the pancreas/depletion of enzymes from exhaustion or overwork can lead to over work of the cells of the pancreas)

Pancreas

Metabolic enzyme potential - the non-digestive enzymes that facilitate chemical reactions in all the cells, including the brain, muscle, nerve, gonads and other tissues - has been shown to decrease significantly in older animals, as compared to younger animals. The implications of this research are that one's life span is determined in large part by the rate at which one's enzyme potential is depleted. Thus, eating raw foods and avoiding over eating are two ways to extend one's enzyme potential, one's health, and perhaps even one's life.

Vitamins

Vitamins are nutrients that our body cannot synthesize, vitamins are in all foods, but each food contains different proportions of vitamins. Vitamins serve as substrates, cofactor and catalysts to many chemical reactions that occur in every cell.

Vitamins: **(A, C, E)** function as antioxidants, protecting other molecules in cells, cell membranes and the blood stream, from the damaging effects of free radicals. Free radical damage has been implicated in arteriosclerosis, cancer and the aging process.

Foods rich in vitamins and minerals must be eaten every day.

Minerals

Major minerals in the body are:
Sodium, potassium, calcium, phosphorous and magnesium, with calcium being the most abundant. These minerals make up the bulk of such tissues as bone.

Other minerals in trace amounts:
Zinc, iodine, manganese, copper, chromium, selenium and even arsenic.

Minerals are key components in enzymes which catalyze or facilitate most of the metabolic processes of the body - from muscle contraction, digestion, thinking, feeling.

Supplements

Small amounts of vitamins and minerals are needed to prevent deficiency diseases. Higher amounts may be necessary for optimal functioning. If health is impaired or nutrition substandard, higher doses will be needed. Diets today are comprised of highly processed and refined foods, making them deficient in multiple nutrients.

In fact, even eating a diet high in vegetables, fruits, grains, nuts and seeds with or without meat, fowl, fish or dairy, one is still at risk of nutritional deficiency.

Mineral depletion of most of the soils in this country is due to intensive farming, erosion of top soil, replenishment of only a select few minerals in inorganic fertilizers. Hybridization of crops has inadvertently lead to a decline in nutrient content.

Organic Foods

As our awareness increases of having a healthy body, we begin to realize even our commercially grown food crops are heavily sprayed with chemicals. Some chemicals are used on the soil prior to planting, some chemicals are sprayed to aid harvest, after harvest some crops are exposed to chemicals to prevent bacteria and fungus growth, or to speed ripening. These chemicals remain in the soil and are taken up into the plants.

Organic food crops, grown without the use of synthetic chemicals, would not pose the risk of commercial crops. Check for organically labeled produce grown in accordance with organic methods, or for organic certification.

Vegetarianism

It seems to be a wide spread belief that the vegetarian path is the more healthy path. Indeed, research shows that as a group, vegetarians have less risk of heart disease, cancer of the breast, colon and prostate, diabetes, osteoporosis, diverticulitis, gallstones, and constipation.

Food animals raised by the routine use of antibiotics, hormones and other chemicals results in drug residues which can have deleterious health effects. Effects of poor living conditions of the animal and the death trauma of the animal flesh, seem to have been ignored.

Some people have experienced remarkable health improvement by eliminating animal flesh from their diet. However, there are also some people who do not function well without some animal flesh - either fish or fowl. Therefore, I encourage everyone to be open to his/her body needs and not attached to any one line of thinking.

Acid/Alkaline Balance

The concept of acid-alkaline balance refers to whether a digest food tends toward increasing tissue PH (alkaline), or lowering PH (acid). Although the blood is maintained at a very narrow range of PH (7.35-7.45), residues of digested foods in body fluids retain a charge that can be positive (alkaline) or negative (acid).

Various sources, from naturopathic physicians to psychic Edgar Cayce, have long espoused the health benefits of emphasizing the consumption of alkaline forming foods over acid forming foods. The waste products of cellular metabolism are acidic. Therefore an acid state is associated with a toxic body.

Alkaline foods:
(most fruit, vegetables, raw and cultured dairy products)

Acid foods:
(meat, refined sweets, cheese, butter, ice cream, alcohol, grains, **legumes, non-cultured dairy**)

Food Combining

The importance of avoiding certain combinations of foods is related to the fact that undigested or only partially digested food in the intestinal tract can produce toxins that are absorbed from the colon into the blood stream. This puts additional demand on the other organs of elimination - the liver, kidneys, lungs, and even the skin.

The following principles of food combining used by many people is as follows:

1)   Avoid eating:
        (protein: meat, dairy - carbohydrates: sugar, starch at the same meal)

2)   Avoid eating;
        (sweet and acidic fruits together - i.e. bananas and pineapple)

3)   Avoid eating;
        (fruit and vegetables at the same meal)

Acceptable Food Combinations Include

1)   Protein and leafy or other low carbohydrate vegetable
        (i.e. chicken, fish or legumes - with green salad or steamed greens)

2)   High carbohydrate vegetable and leafy or low carbohydrate vegetable
        (i.e. sweet potato, rice grain - with green salad or steamed greens)

Absorption

Contrary to the opinion you may have formed from the above, eating the **right** foods will not ensure that the necessary nutrients will be absorbed into your body. The amount of nutrients actually absorbed depends on the health integrity and efficient functioning of all organs of digestion.

To fully understand how easily digestion can be disturbed, it is helpful to understand how the sympathetic and parasympathetic nervous systems influence digestion. These two aspects of your autonomic nervous system have opposing actions, and when one is stimulated, the other is deactivated.

Sympathetic Nervous System - controls heart rate, breathing, nerve stimulation and blood flow to skeletal muscles.

Parasympathetic Nervous System - controls secretions of the gastrointestinal tract and peristalsis.

Thus, we can see that eating when upset or rushed will divert blood flow and nerve stimulation away from the digestive organs, causing inadequate salivary, gastric, pancreatic, etc., secretions which affect improper digestion due to lack of enzymes, "weak" enzymes, improper PH, etc. Any step in the process, compromises and limits digestive capacity at all subsequent steps.

The results are:

1) inadequate nutrient absorption
2) altered bowel micro-organism with decreased beneficial bacteria, and increased growth of non-beneficial and potentially pathogenic micro-organisms, including yeast
3) depressed immune function
4) generation and absorption of toxins
5) build-up of toxic load in the body
6) increased burden on the organs of elimination

Chronic mal-digestion and mal-absorption will prevent the digestive organs and tissue from receiving the nutrients they require to fulfill their function. This eventually leads to tissue changes, pathology and diagnosable illness.

Elimination

All cellular processes produce waste products which are toxic to the body. These wastes must be carried out of the body continuously. The colon, liver, kidneys, lungs, and skin are the major organs of elimination. Without their proper functioning, toxins build-up in tissues and biochemical imbalances occur, leading to impaired function and eventual pathology. Intentional cleansing practices must be a part of any therapy for chronic disease as well as disease prevention and purification.

A healthy life-style will encompass the following guidelines:

1) low fat - especially avoid fried foods, hydrogenated oil, refined oils
2) limit animal flesh consumption - fish and fowl are preferable to red meat
3) eat a variety of fresh raw vegetables daily (5-6 servings)
4) eat a variety of fresh raw fruit daily (3-4 servings)
5) minimum of 2 quarts of pure water daily, preferably between meals
6) avoid chemicals and preservatives like MSG, nitrites, nitrates in processed foods
7) avoid empty calorie foods like soda and candy
8) avoid stimulants like caffeine, sugar and other drugs
9) chew food thoroughly - chew solids until liquid, chew liquids as if they were solid
10) eat in a relaxed atmosphere and calm state of mind
11) avoid over eating
12) insurance: supplement the diet with cultures of acidophilus and intestinal bacteria
      (i.e. yogurt with live cultures)

UNDERSTANDING DETOXIFICATION
by Claire Zieman

The Law of Cure

"All cure starts from within out, and from the head down, and in reverse order as the symptoms have appeared."   - Christine Hering - Homeopath

How important this is to accept and realize. There are no quick fixes, no immediate reversals. Healing takes time, effort, intent, and knowledge. Lets take a look at how we can bring our bodies into balance and the processes we go through.

Renowned Nutritionist Dr. Bernard Jensen defines the process as follows:

Detoxification: relates to reduction of toxic materials in the body, and to making this toxic material easier to be eliminated. Therefore, the first part of my health program involves enabling the body to begin rejecting materials collected in the years before from bad diet and poor health habits.

Reversal Process: is the retracing of the stages or steps of each disease you have had, reactivating each one and eliminating it. Many people who have suppressed diseases all their lives think an elimination, such as a cold, is a sickness instead of a healing process.

Healing Crisis: follows the Reversal Process. It is an effort on all organs to become new and strong again. Though it may feel like a disease crisis, it will not last as long, or develop into another disease. Instead, it will bring about renewed health.

Catarrh, Phlegm and Mucus: are a termination process of toxic materials, acid and debris which the body does not want. It can be the end result of the body tissues breaking down and has to find a way out of the body. The accumulation of this material can be eliminated through any orifice, skin or any of the eliminative organs.

The **naturopathic** school of thought distinguishes between a "healing crisis" and a "disease crisis". They may look similar on the outside but they are taking place under completely different conditions.

Disease Crisis: is when the body has reached its tolerance level with toxins and waste production. The bodies defense brings forth an elimination of toxins, in the form of cold, fever, etc. The body is on the defensive and produces a dis-ease crisis.

How do we detoxify and what is included: The bowels, lungs, kidneys, skin and lymphatic system are all eliminates. On an average, two pounds of toxins are eliminated from each organ daily.

The kidney, skin and liver all detoxify. The liver at any given time contains one fourth of your blood. It is imperative for you to keep it cleansed. Alcohol causes liver damage and will interfere with liver function. When the liver functions correctly - bile is sent into the colon stimulating bowel movement.

The Colon

The colon has the poorest nerve supply in the body. One half of all our bowel movement is the body breaking down, not what we eat. That is why juice fasting, juicing and six to eight glasses of water a day are so important to optimal health. The main elements for proper bowel function include: calcium, potassium and magnesium. Chewing food well assists saliva into the stomach making it less acidic. Bowel cleanses, psyllium husks, and colon hydro-therapy will attempt to cleanse the colon.

Colon hydro-therapy: is a safe, restorative procedure which gently infuses warm, filtered water into the colon without discomfort to the individual. The entire colon is thereby cleansed - stress free.

A healthy colon is essential to a healthy body. Today's diet is all too often composed of saturated fats, processed, refined and devitalized foods. This contributes to problems associated with the large intestines - colitis, constipation, diarrhea and toxemia, to name just a few. Eliminating undigested food particles, glandular and cellular debris, excess mucous, gas and parasites is an essential part of the digestive and assimilative processes.

Increases in environmental pollutants, such as pesticides, herbicides, and preservatives; as well as antibiotics, chemical and hormonal food additives heighten the need for these "toxins" to be removed from the body. Additionally, bacterial toxicity results from waste material which remains in, and stagnates in the colon.

Many of these toxins are re-absorbed into the blood stream, lymph, liver and nervous system; thus straining and eventually weakening the body's defense against viruses and foreign bacteria. The result is a breakdown which affects the body as a whole.

Cleansing helps provide therapeutic improvement of colon muscle-tone, necessary for peristalsis. It also cleanses, and dilutes the toxin load in the colon, resulting in a reduced burden on the liver. In turn, this helps restore internal balance and improves overall health by supporting the eliminative organs and rejuvenating the immune system.

In the **Edgar Cayce Handbook for Health Through Drugless Therapy**, Harold J. Reilly says "Colon hydro-therapy together with castor oil packs and manipulation, are truly the distinctive hallmark of the Cayce drugless therapy".

Skin will eliminate toxins: by sweating, body odor, acne, boils, acne. The list goes on. Skin brushing every morning will help stimulate the skin and open the pores, aiding the release of toxins such as uric acid crystals and catarrh. Wearing natural fibers will allow your skin to breathe. You make new skin every twenty four hours. Our bodies are truly amazing!

Exercise of the Lungs

The lungs are a channel through which the air we breathe passes so that the blood can collect the oxygen and nitrogen needed to keep us alive. Tobacco is harmful to the lungs as it destroys and damages the alveoli of the lungs. As stated by Norman Walker "The condition of the entire breathing apparatus depends on the cleanliness of the colon, as well as the lungs. Fermentation and putrecation in the colon have their effect on the health of every part of the anatomy".

Exercise helps the lungs to breathe. There are many types of breath work therapy available to assist with this process. The mini-trampoline is particularly beneficial. "Physical fitness is a measure of circulation efficiency. Increase circulation efficiency of the body fluids - the lymphatic and the blood stream that services the cells - and the body is considered physically fit. The muscles are able to continue the same work longer without fatigue." (Albert E. Carter)

When using the mini-trampoline to strengthen every cell in our body, it is important to remember that the feet do not leave the mat. Deep breathing is also necessary. As we begin to clear the body, unprocessed metabolic waste in tissues and undigested food accumulates in the system.. As the waste empties, it becomes circulating fluid called lymph.

Kidney Function

1) regulates water and electrolyte content
2) maintains an acid/base equilibrium
3) eliminates metabolic waste products
4) retains vital substances

The kidneys are complex and their work is nothing short of amazing! As cells and tissues of the body use food and oxygen, they produce waste. Carbon dioxide is eliminated through the lungs while the kidneys extract waste of protein metabolism in the form of urea and uric acid. The kidneys also extract cast-off used up minerals, other elements, and waste water from the lymph stream and from the blood.

One of the easiest most helpful means of caring for the kidneys is drinking water. Six to eight glasses a day does wonders for your system. Especially important is to have a glass as soon as you wake in the morning. This will aid your system and help rid it of urine which has been there all night. It will also help develop muscle tone.

These are just a few suggestions to help you, remember only you can take care of you!!

The following four pages on **Vitamin and Herb Reference Charts** are from Dr. Albert Zehr's book *"Healthy Steps"* (see Bibliography Section for publishing information)

Vitamin Reference Chart

Abbreviations

Acid — Acidophilus
Adren — Adrenal Stimulant
   Formula †
Cal — Calcium
Dig —Digestive Supplement †
FGlan — Female Multi Glandular †
Lec — Lecithin

MGlan — Male Multi Glandular†
Min — Chelated Multi Mineral†
Multi — Multi Vitamin Mineral †
PA — Pantothenic Acid
Pot — Potassium
Pro — Protein
Sel — Selenium

Acne	E, A, B6, PA, Zinc	Eczema	Niacin, B, B6, Multi
Arteries	A, B6, C, E, Multi, Sel	Eyes	A, C, E, PA, B, Pro
		Fingernails	Pro, A, Cal
Arthritis	B, C, E, Calcium, PA, Pro, Multi	Flu	C, E, B6, B, Multi
		Gout	B, C, E, PA, Min
Asthma	PA, C, A, E, Adren	Hair	Pro, B, Multi, Zinc
Backache	C, Cal, Pro, Min	Kidney Stones	Cal, B6, Min, C
Bed Sores	B Complex	Liver	Pro, A,C,E,B,Min
Blood Clotting	C, E, Cal,Min	Motion Sickness	B6, B
— Inhibits Clotting	Pro, E, C, Lec, Multi	Muscular Cramps	B6, Cal, PA, Multi, Adren
Blood Pressure		Nervousness	B, Cal, Min, B6
— High	C, E, Multi, Lec, Sel, Pot	Nosebleeds	C
		Ovaries	C, Min, Fe Glan
— Low	B, C, E, PA, Pro, Sel	Prostate	A, C, Min, Zinc, MGlan
Bruising	C		
Burns	B, C, E	Psoriasis	B6, Lec, A
Canker Sores	B6, Niacin, B	Sinus	A, B6, C, E, PA
Cholesterol	A. B6, C, E,Lec, Multi	Stretch Marks	E, PA
		Throat, Sore	C, B
Cold Sores	PA, C, B6	Ulcers	A, B, C, E, PA
Colds	PA, C, B, Min	Varicose Veins	B, C, E, Lec, Min
Colitis	Multi, PA, Min		
Constipation	Multi, B, E, PA	Warts	A, E
Diarrhea	B6, B, Niacin,Multi, Pot	Wrinkles	B6, E, A
Digestion	Acid, Dig, A, B, C, E, Lec		

(From the book *"Healthy Steps"* by Dr. Albert Zehr)

Diabetes	Dandelion , Golden Seal, Spirulina, Uva Ursi
Diarrhea	Mullein, Thyme, White Oak Bark
Digestive Disorders	Alfalfa, Barley Green, Bee Pollen, Garlic, Wood Betony
Drug WIthdrawal	Chamomile,
Drugs, Resistance to	Ginseng
Ears	Chickweed, Garlic, Lobelia, Yellow Dock
Eyes	Eyebright, Spirulina
Fatigue	Bee Pollen, Garlic, Ginseng, Gotu Kola,
Female Complaints	Black Cohosh, Damiana, Licorice , Uva Ursi
Female Hormone Imbalance	Damiana, Sarsaparilla
Fever	Chamomile, Safflower
Flu	Capsicum, Ginger
Gallbladder	Safflower, Cascara Sagrada
Gas	Ginger, Sarsaparilla, Thyme
Hair, Nails, Teeth	Horsetail
Headache	Ginger, Thyme, White Willow , Wood Betony
Heart	Capsicum, Hawthorne Berry, Mullein,
Hemmorrhoids	Mullein, White Oak Bark
Hypoglycemia	see Blood Sugar — Low
Impotency	see Sexual Debility
Infection	Echinacea, Garlic, Golden Seal
Insomnia	Chamomile, Valerian
Intestinal Tract — Inflamation	Licorice Root
Kidney	Alfalfa, Barley Green, Capsicum, Horse-tail, Uva Ursi
Lead removal	Barley Green, Spirulina
Liver	Barley Green, Chaparral, Dandelion Safflower, Spirulina, Yellow Dock
Lungs	Chickweed, Lobelia, Mullein
Lymphatics	Chaparral,
Membranes — inflamation	Chickweed, Comfrey, Golden Seal,
Menstrual Pain	Black Cohosh, White Oak Bark

(From the book *"Healthy Steps"* by Dr. Albert Zehr)

Menstrual Flow	
— excessive	Uva Ursi
— stimulation	Chamomile, Thyme
Mercury removal	Barley Green, Spirulina
Motion Sicknes	Ginger,
Muscles — Cramps	Safflower
— Spasms	Valerian
Nervous Disorders	Chamomile, Gotu Kola, Thyme, Valerian, Wood Betony
Obesity	Chickweed, Kelp, Poke Root
Pain	Mullein, Valerian, White Willow Bark
Pancreas	Dandelion, Spirulina, Uva Ursi
Parasites	Black Walnut Leaves, Garlic, Sarsaparilla, Wood Betony
Poison, Resistance to	Barley Green, Ginseng, Sarsaparilla,
Prostate disease	Bee Pollen, Echinacea, Kelp
Psoriasis	Dandelion, Sarsaparilla, Yellow Dock
Radiation	Ginseng, Spirulina
Respiratory	Comfrey, Lobelia, Mullein,
Rheumatism	Capsicum, Poke Root, Sarsaparilla, Yucca
Senility	Gotu Kola
Sexual Debility	Bee Pollen, Damiana, Licorice Root, Ginseng
Skin	Horsetail, Sarsaparilla, Yellow Dock, Yucca
Spleen	Dandelion , Poke Root, Uva Ursi
Stimulant	Capsicum,
Stomach — upset	Chamomile, Ginger
Stress	Lobelia,
Throats, sore	Bee Pollen, Garlic, Ginger, Licorice, White Oak
Thyroid	Kelp, Poke Root
Tumors	Chaparral, Chickweed, Echinacea, Yellow Dock
Ulcers	Capsicum, Licorice, Spirulina, Yellow Dock
Urethral Tract	Chaparral, Uva Ursi
Varicose Veins	Black Walnut, Capsicum, White Oak Bark
Viral Infections	Echinacea, Safflower, Uva Ursi

(From the book *"Healthy Steps"* by Dr. Albert Zehr)

Herb Reference Chart

(See also Chapter 13: Herbal Combinations)

Acne	Barley Green, Bee Pollen, Chaparral, Yellow Dock
Adrenal Glands	Licorice Root
Aging	Bee Pollen, Ginseng, Gotu Kola
Allergies	Barley Green, Bee Pollen, Spirulina,
Anemia	Alfalfa, Comfrey, Dandelion,Spirulina, Yellow Dock
Appetite Depresant	Chickweed,
Arthritis	Alfalfa, Barley Green, Capsicum, Chaparral, Poke Root,Sarsaparilla, Yucca
Asthma	Black Cohosh, Lobelia, Mullein, Thyme
Atherosclerosis	Hawthorne Berry
Bladder	Alfalfa, Horsetail,Uva Ursi
Blood — oxygenation	Black Walnut Leaves
— purifier	Chaparral, Dandelion, Echinacea, Poke Root, Sarsaparilla, Yellow Dock, Yucca
Blood Pressure	
— high	Barley Green, Dandelion, Garlic, Hawthorne Berry, Evening Primrose
Blood Pressure — low	Hawthorn Berry
Blood Sugar — balance	Black Walnut Leaves,
Blood Sugar — low	Hawthorne Berry, Licorice Root
Bones, broken	Comfrey, Horsetail
Bronchials	Chamomile,Comfrey, Ginger, Lobelia, Thyme
Chemotherapy	Spirulina
Childbirth	Black Cohosh,
Circulation	Capsicum, Ginger
Colds	Capsicum, Garlic, Ginger, Licorice Root, Safflower, Golden Seal
Colic	Chamomile, Wood Betony
Constipation	Cascara Sagrada,
Coughs	Ginger, Licorice Root, Lobelia, Thyme
Cramps — stomach	Barley Green, Black Walnut Leaves, Ginger, Wood Betony

Acid-Forming & Alkaline-Forming Foods

Note:
Because a food is acid is no indication that it <u>remains</u> acid in the body - it can turn alkaline. Honey or raw sugar produces alkaline ash, because a high concentrate of sugar becomes acid-formers. One should eat 80% alkaline to 20% acid for best health. The following *fruit-foods should <u>not</u> be eaten with other foods.

Alkaline Fruits
apples
apricots
avocados
bananas
berries -all
cantaloupe
cherries
currants
dates
figs
grapes
grapefruit*
kumquats*
lemons* - ripe
limes*
mangos
nectarines
olives
oranges*
papayas
passion fruit
peaches
pears
persimmons
pineapple
plums
pomegranates
melons - all
prunes
raisins
tangerines*
tomatoes

Acid Fruits
all preserves
all canned fruits
cranberries
dried-sulphered
olives -pickled

Alkaline Vegetables
alfalfa sprouts
artichokes

asparagus
bamboo shoots
beans/ green,
wax/string/lima
beets
broccoli
cabbages
carrots
celery
cauliflower
chard
coconut
corn
cucumber
dill
eggplant
endive
escarole
garlic
horseradish
artichokes
kale
leeks
lettuce
mushrooms
okra
onions
parsley
parsnips
peppers - bell
potatoes
pumpkin
radish
romaine lettuce
rutabagas
sauerkraut
soybeans
spinach
sprouts
squash
sweet potatoes
turnips
water chestnuts
watercress
yams

Acid Vegetables
asparagus tips
beans - dried
brussel sprouts
garbanzos
lentils
rhubarb

Alkaline Dairy
acidophilus milk
buttermilk
yogurt
milk - raw
whey

Acid Dairy
butter
cheese - all
cottage cheese
cream
custards
margarine
milk/boiled
cooked/malted/
dried

Alkaline Misc.
coffee substitute
honey
kelp
tea - herbal

Acid Misc.
alcoholic drinks
cocoa
coffee
condiments - all
dressings
drugs
eggs
flavorings
mayonnaise
tapioca
teas

tobacco
vinegar
lack of sleep

**Foods
High in Copper**
American cheese
sweet potatoes
dry lima beans
dried prunes
citrus fruits
beef liver
pork chops
dried peas
mushrooms
white bread
mackerel
dry beans
whole rye
chocolate
asparagus
almonds
avocado
cabbage
chicken & beef
kale
lobster
grapes
flour
oats
pecans
oysters
shrimp
spinach
turkey
walnuts
wheat
eggs
apples
bananas
corn
carrots

Foods
High in Calcium
green vegetables
mustard greens
turnip greens
egg yolk
shellfish
broccoli
kale soybeans
milk/dairy prod.
canned:
sardines & salmon

Foods
High in Iron
dark molasses
dry apricots
wheat germ
liver sausage
legumes - all
dried beans
soy beans
lean meats
eggs - yolk
dried fruits
green-
leafy vegetables
grain cereals
cocoa
peaches
nuts
shellfish/seafoods

Foods High
in Manganese
whole:
grain rye-
wheat flour
sweet potatoes
snap beans
whole corn
white flour
dried peas
dried prunes
white rice
liver
oatmeal
wheat
spinach
bananas
beets
lettuce
kale
dry beans

raw tomatoes
lima beans
raw carrots
roasted poultry
citrus fruits
brown rice
peaches
potatoes
soy flour
barley
cocoa
nuts:
brazil, hazelnuts
walnuts, almonds
cashews, peanuts

Foods
High in Zinc
peanut butter
canned pears
canned cherries
rice cereal
maple syrup
wheat bran
oatmeal
dry yeast
whole corn
rye bread
cows milk
oysters
wheat bread
can applesauce
rice
peas
eggs
beets
cabbage
wheat & barley
spinach
carrots
clams
herrings
lettuce

Foods High
in Potassium
buttermilk
swiss cheese
cow milk
goat milk
blackberries
blueberries
red currants
red raspberries

dried apricots
brussel sprouts
dandelion greens
mustard greens
turnip greens
raw, dry beans
bran flakes
wheat flakes
puffed wheat
dark rye flour
cauliflower
corn bread
roasted nuts
cooked meats
seafoods
chicken
chocolate

Foods
High in Potassium
molasses
brown sugar
citrus fruits - all
citrus juices - all
dried fruit:
dates, figs,
prunes, raisins
raw beets
raw carrots
raw parsnips
raw potatoes
radishes
raw turnips
asparagus
beet greens
raw cabbage
avocados
kale
bananas
cherries
parsley
spinach
artichoke
wild rice
broccoli
okra
wheat germ
sweet corn
lentils
peas
pumpkin
soybeans
catsup
wheat bread

Foods High
in Sodium
graham crackers
cheddar cheese
cottage cheese
evap. milk
french dressing
popped corn
canned:
fish, crab
carrots,
asparagus
sauerkraut,
spinach, peas
baked beans
lima beans
mushrooms
tomato catsup
potato chips
hot dogs
chipped beef
cream cheese
rye & wheat bread
butter
buttermilk
saltines
pretzels
bacon
bologna
cured ham
liverwurst
corned beef
olives
flakes:
rye, bran,
corn, rice
& wheat
white bread

Acid Flesh Food
all meats:
fowl, fish
shellfish
jello, gelatin

Alkaline Nuts
almonds
chestnuts - roasted
coconut - fresh

Acid Nuts
nuts/except above
coconut - dried

NOTES:

SYMBOLS AND THEIR EMPOWERMENT

The process of receiving an attunement is through the scientific language of symbols, and comes from ancient Tibet. This language of symbols was rediscovered in the mid-nineteenth century by Japanese scholar Dr. Mikao Usui.

Attunement:

The Reiki attunement is taught by the Reiki Master to the student. The attunement process opens the chakras and creates that special link between the one receiving, and the universal life force energy, the source of Reiki.

The Reiki attunement for an individual is a powerful spiritual experience. The attunements open gateways to wholeness and the sense of totality. The attunement process is guided by the (Rei) divine consciousness; and is directed according to each student's needs.

Some experiences by students include: warm fuzzy feelngs of being wrapped in a blanket of energy, feeling very connected to divine consciousness, tears of wholeness and belonging, opening of the third eye, healings, acute intuitive awareness, personal messages, past life experiences, a sense of being part of the whole, life's work, and visions. Each student connects to their own mystical experience.

Once your Reiki attunement has been placed in your field of energy, the initiation is always with you. The process of receiving an attunement is based on truth and mysticism. How much the attunements benefit you is partly based upon your being open to receive. Believe in yourself. Know that truth is Oneness, but the paths are many. Being open to the belief system of Reiki is opening yourself to divine consciousness, regardless of whether you can put a label on it!

Symbols and You:

Symbols influence your body's energy and physical being on the levels of mental, emotional, physical and spiritual. The Symbols are a reminder of the divine power within each person - that becomes activated upon receipt of an attunement. The Symbols can be used for send: healing, empowering yourself, your surroundings, meditation, plants, animals, children, peacefulness, protection, harmony and balance.

On the following pages - spaces are provided for the symbols given during your training.

The Power Symbol:

The power symbol charges and boosts the Reiki energy flow. This symbol is used to focus the energy around the clients while giving a treatment as well as to clear the room before any spiritual seminars or bodywork massage, etc.   Using this symbol helps create a sacred energized space to work.

Power symbols can also boost the energy around newly planted trees, protect your mode of transportation, pets and home, etc. You can direct energy out into the divine consciousness for specified areas of healing: (i.e.- Rain Forests, famine, weather disasters, war, troubled parts of the globe, etc.)

This symbol is used as protection on the levels of physical and verbal protection as well as emotional and spiritual protection. Other uses include: blessing your food, cleansing your water before drinking and blessing your clients before a treatment. *Intention* - sending this power symbol forward, as in *Beaming* Reiki energy is the important point.

You can protects your property, your belongings, your meditation area, your garden or yourself driving down the highway. You can send this energy forward if you see an accident along the road, traffic jams, etc. Do all of this with a blessing of unconditional love and intention of good will.

This is your Pathway of Light - your decree of unconditional love to one planet ♥ one people.

Notes:

Mental & Emotional Symbol:

This symbol is used to balance the right and left side of the brain, it represents "God and Man" coming together in harmony and peace. Useful in any emotional or mental situation, (i.e. - psychic counseling, ministers' work, fear, anger, depression, sadness, relationships). This symbol works out of the areas of the Heart-emotional chakra and the Solar Plexus-mental chakra, jointly working together for the harmony and balance of the client.

The symbol can also be used for addictions: (i.e. - smoking, weight loss, drinking or drugs).

The use of this symbol is helpful when you have misplaced an item. It works with the subconscious mind and brings to the surface what is needed. When you are meditating and doing affirmations or when you are working with a difficult work situation, this symbol will help balance out the energies in these situations.

For long term goals of change such as smoking or weight loss, write the unwanted habit, your name, a healthy result and the symbol on paper. Keep this in a place where you can send energy on a daily basis for (21 days). You can put it under a crystal or in your medicine bag. After the 21 days, burn the paper and send the energy out to the universe for total healing and release. The best release time would be three days before a New Moon cycle.

You are in a state of grace when using this symbol
Recovering and regaining your sense of pure spirit
- The Spiritual Warrior -

Notes:

Distant Healing Symbol:

This symbol is used for absentee healing. Sending Reiki (universal life force energy) out to others at a distance. The symbol is a blessing and represents the *Power of the Universe, Bestowing the Truth;* and transcends time and space.

The symbol creates finding the true Oneness, which connects with our essence bringing about the Light and (the wisdom), the connection. The symbol can be used to prepare a room for meditation, healing, massage, treatments, counseling or any psychic work..

It is used with the power and mental & emotional symbols when beaming energy, doing your prayer list, traveling, aiding hospital patients, friends or relatives that live away from you, etc.

The Distant Symbol is bridging time and space. You can send this energy forward in time, into the future with the proper intention. It can be used if you are going in for hospital testing, have a court case, important meetings, dentist appointments, etc.

The symbol is representative of - The Wand - The Blessing

Notes:

GROUP DISTANT HEALING

Distant healing can be sent by any group of like minded individuals as long as the intention is focused by the group, (i.e. - Goddess healing groups, Medicine Wheel ceremonies, Healing and Prayer groups, Reiki Open House groups, etc.)

The method commonly used is:
a) form a circle of people and send the Reiki energy into the circle
b) the inside/middle/center of the circle is the vortex or spiral point
c) using the power symbol, the mental-emotional symbol and the distant symbol - focus the energy into the center of the circle
d) pictures/photographs can be placed within the circle for healing
e) names can be called out for healing energy - including your own
f) energies can be sent out for planetary or global conditions
g) all of this sends out to the universe the vibrations for those in need
h) you can sing, chant, or drum
I) intention is for the best interest and highest good of those receiving
j) remember, where one or more are gathered together in His name - there is an endless source of divine energy

EMPOWERING YOUR GOALS

If you have a pet project, or a global environmental goal you are working with, you can use the Reiki healing symbols. In the last 50 years since Reiki has been reintroduced, we have become aware of the potential that the Reiki techniques offer. Use of the Reiki symbols gives you the opportunity of reaching out - of directing the healing energies - of becoming a part of the re-creation. How exciting to know you are part of the adventure and myth - take the challenge!

Help in the making of one planet ♥ one people . . .

For personal goals or goals that may be blocked:

1) write your name on a piece of paper
2) write your goals on this paper
3) draw the symbols on the paper
4) work daily with this goal by energizing with Reiki - for 21 days
5) try connecting with the earth in a new and deeper way
6) surround yourself with **unconditional love** and harmony - you will strengthen your energy flow, dissolving the emotional conflict at the subconscious level
7) at the end of 21 days, burn the paper and release out to the universe - good release time - approximately three days before a new moon

One Planet ♥♥♥♥ One People

10 LEVELS OF CONSCIOUSNESS SYMBOL

This symbol reawakens your memory. It is a massage of the soul, a soul memory retrieval, going beyond the fears or limits of man. It is remembrance of no beginning and no end, the foreverness.

The words/definitions or translation working with this symbol act as a catalyst of going outward and inward at the same time - the foreverness of who and what we are in the universe.

1) _________________________   ____

2) _________________________   ____

3) _________________________   ____

4) _________________________   ____

5) _________________________   ____

6) _________________________   ____

7) _________________________   ____

8) _________________________   ____

9) _________________________   ____

10) ________________________   ____

Technique and Notes:

Usui Master Symbol

Tibetan Master Symbol

Tibetan Energy Symbol

Notes:

GOLDEN LIGHT ALIGNMENT

The Golden Light Alignment was revealed in a mystic experience where three channelers had gathered together to work with Divine Source. They were not asking for or expecting the information that was given to them. "We thought we had gathered together to do healing work on the Eastern coastline - but were open for a different experience." Direction was given to "open the pathway" for *many peoples* in the future days. The changes in vibrational energies on our planet are effecting us all. With these changes the Brotherhood of Light, Angelic Ones and Rainbow Warriors are "working with" many Lightworkers in different ways, opening the doorway for our planet earth on her voyage of evolution.

Helping us in the acknowledgment and acceptance of : One Planet ♥ One People

The symbols are ancient and from many cultures, incorporating our past, present and beyond into one.

Symbol One: **Symbol Two:**

Notes:

Symbol Three:

Symbol Four:

Symbol Five:

Symbol Six:

Symbol Seven:

Symbol Eight:

One Planet ♥♥♥♥♥ One People

My Initiation

My knees felt weak as I descended the stairs from the initiation room upstairs to the living room where our class was being held. The other members waited with anticipation for their turn. As I settled onto the sofa, relieved to sit and catch my breath, someone asked "How was it?" "Profound", I responded.

Profound was the only word which came to mind at that moment. It is the only word which can describe what was an intensely personal and spiritual experience. I was affected physically, emotionally and psychologically at the moment of initiation. Things moved. I felt a spectrum of emotions from joy to despair to relief, pain and disappointment in a single moment. It was cleansing. I felt the movement of Kundulini so intense that it caused me to jump in my seat. There was breath which hit me in my solar plexus so hard that it left me gasping. It was movement. Then there was the feeling of uncompromising love, so emcompassing that it made me giddy and left me trembling. It was enlightenment.

What followed for days after was as important as the initial experience. For the initiation into Reiki does not end when one walks out of the initiation. I began viewing the world and those around me differently. My psychic abilities were highly tuned up. I was extremely tuned into events, thoughts and the people around me. It left me feeling as though I was finally emerging out of a dark tunnel into the light of day after a long period of confinement. My dreams became very intense and vivid. Tangible dreams about "unfinished" business. These dreams were usually about people and events which had less than positive memories for me. They brought closure and peace to many "issues" which I had been shoved to the back of my consciousness. I would wake up remembering my dreams, which is unusual for me.

People around me also noticed a change, I was different. Overnight, I had become a more patient and positive person. My enthusiasm at work place was noticeable. I was less likely to complain and criticize and more willing to go the extra mile; more productive. That has continued and can not be explained by my supervisor.

I have since learned that each person after experiencing the power and love which is Reiki - experiences an adjustment period after their initiation. My experiences are unique to me and my connection to God, as well as the road which brought me to seek the knowledge to use Reiki. No other person will ever experience exactly the same thing on initiation. Opening to the healing power which is Reiki, has empowered me, given me strength and foresight, and changed my life in many subtle wonderful ways. I look forward to the road on which I travel and the lessons which I will encounter on my journey to enlightenment.

Ruth Hutton

One Planet ♥♥♥♥ One People

Notes:

Beginning Visions

When is was suggested to me to take the Reiki Healing Classes, my thoughts were, "What in the world is that?" I had been to various other classes in my search along the spiritual pathway, (my pathway is really really new!!) so I thought, "What would Reiki do for me"?

Sitting in the Reiki class, I seemed to be following what was happening, but I didn't quite make the connection. When I attended the second day my awareness had sharpened and something seemed to click in me; lights went off in my head. What was all that?! I was in a daze, not sure what feelings were going through my mind. A few days later my awareness came like a <u>flash</u>! My opinion is that Reiki is different for everyone. Your process, your attunement, your initiation is a special part of you and your divine source; and what happens is yours and yours alone. For me, the healing experience is very warming and intense; a far cry from the personal belief that I would ever be interested in any healing work.

The understanding I have received with Reiki has since developed into finding the inner peace and strength within myself. My awareness was heightened, I felt unconditional love, visions became clear and more prominent on a daily basis.

During our Reiki Clinics or Reiki Open House groups, I have realized I can be helpful with these visions. I thought everyone saw what I saw. It was really exciting for me to share seeing the body grids, body parts, colors and the energy proceeding throughout the body for healing. I am grateful for the encouragement of my friends who talked me into these classes, and now for knowing I have found my place in the scheme of life. I am looking forward to helping others in their understanding of what their bodies say to them, how the energy moves through them, healing their bodies and minds as one. Life is sweet.

Brenda Stone

BEYOND EXPERIENCES

Healing - A Symbiotic Relationship

The Divine powers, whatever or whomever they may be, must look down on us with a mixture of mirth and sadness. We were designed, and created to be perfect in all aspects. This includes mental, physical and emotional health. Mother Nature is a perfectionist -- the original perfectionist whose powers created and set the Cosmos into motion and into life.

We say we enjoy good health; some of us even profess to be "health nuts," though using more flattering terms. As a society, we are becoming more conscious of our environment, our habits, our social surroundings, and our attitudes. Yet, little of this translates to our health.

Isn't that amazing? We can use all the things we have learned about being "Earth Friendly" to our streets and our beaches without realizing we are in control of our own inner environment as much, if not more so.

The ancients knew what we have either forgotten or ignored, that our bodies can take care of themselves if we allow them to do so. We read of miracles in the <u>Readers Digest</u> each month, forgetting that each healed cut, each complex carbohydrate converted, each movement from darkness into enlightenment is also a miracle.

Would Mother Nature, who created a universe that may never run down, create imperfect life and then give it the intelligence to realize how hopeless existence was? I would certainly hope not, and suggest some ways to realize a more perfect relationship with that universal power, Divine power if you wish, to gain and keep a healthy mind in a healthy body for so long as you choose to do so.

In real estate, it is said, there are three important factors to consider before purchasing property: location, location and location. Well, the metaphysical analogy to that is, there are three important factors to consider in ensuring good health - attitude; attitude and attitude. Certainly there is more to it than that, as there are other factors to consider in real estate besides location, but attitude is a founding, pivotal factor which is absolutely necessary. We are never without attitude, just as a piece of property is never without location. It is always somewhere, good or bad; the property exists somewhere. Well, good or bad, we always have an attitude.

How many of you reading this get up in the morning appreciating - truly and sincerely appreciating - the opportunity to traverse yet another day in this reality called life on Earth? How many of you refuse to use the expression, "What'd ya expect, it's Monday"? Those are set-ups to failure. Those are set-ups to ill feelings, to emotional lows and, subsequently, to headaches, stomach disorders and general feelings of low energy.

Many of you, on the other hand, know the exhilarating experience of waking up in the morning, full of 'vim and vigor,' ready to accept and achieve any challenge that may come your way. You are appreciative of yet another day to live and enjoy the gifts, the miracles, of life all around you. It doesn't matter if the sun is shining, or if a hurricane is going on around you -- that day, the one you are about to begin, is a box to be filled with exciting learning and living experiences.

The attitudes described in the immediately preceding paragraph belong to people who are more likely to find headaches and other 'routine' aches and pains at a minimum. When they are ill, it is not for long, and even then they listen to their bodies and provide for their immediate needs.

There is so much common sense involved in taking care of yourself. It's as simple as covering up if you're cold and drinking when you are thirsty. It's as complex as realizing that the billions of cells in your body are able to improve themselves in accordance with your wishes.

Those of you reading this who are healers, traditional or nontraditional healers, know that a patient's attitude is an essential factor in his or her recovery. Case studies have shown that recovery is affected by many supposedly non-medical factors: what are the practitioners saying as they treat the patient, the experience level of hope in the patient, the expression of hope by the practitioners, and even the music played during treatment and recovery. Amazing isn't it?

This article is not meant to be a how-to of good health. It's intention is to get you, the reader, interested in exploring your own attitudes and to experience how differing outlooks on the same situations influence their outcomes. Watch yourself as you go through each day; observe those around you who navigate through each day with differing attitudes. Then use those observations to improve your own outlook and daily attitudes. Become a helper to your healing, to your chosen healer. Open up to the possibility that your body WANTS to be healthy, and that the only person capable of stopping the healing is YOU!

Archie Whitehill

Reiki - On a Larger Scale - Your Planet

Reiki to heal a planet?? What a ridiculous thought. How in the world (pun intended) can we save a planet, our earth, by a simple Reiki healing technique? Well, that's a good question, and one that needs to be asked.

In order to answer it, I need first to say, there are a growing number of people who believe that we have to heal ourselves first. Then changes will occur that will in fact heal the planet. We need to change our patterns' of thought. We need to unite in prayer and action. If you have action and intent, you get reaction. I'm not talking about a bunch of people getting together and praying the earth heals. You can't think pollution away; or move mountains of trash through meditation. You can, however, generate positive ideas through both.

With positive nurturing ideas comes action. If action is for the good and betterment of our environment, the reaction is earth healing. If you "think" you'll plant a tree, that's a good idea, a positive thought. It starts there. When you plant the tree, you've taken action - positive action. When the tree grows, it is a reaction to your action of planting it. It becomes manifest. It is!

The reaction doesn't stop there. That single tree has its effect on the environment, which in turn also reacts. All of this started with an idea. If you get enough people planting trees, you'll soon have a forest.

Through Reiki, we aren't planting trees in the literal sense. The seeds being planted are healing our minds, bodies and spirits. Putting us in contact with each other on a very intimate level of truly caring about another person and knowing we can cause a reaction through action. We may not even know the person, or about their life, what they do, or even their name. They are important to us and the intimacy is on a much higher level; a spiritual level. We don't have to know you, to care that you are.

Through Reiki, we seem to start caring on a different, more expansive level. Becoming in tune to this "life force" and recognizing this in people leads to "seeing" it in all things. The Native Americans knew and reacted with the "life force". Their respect for the environment and knowledge that certain procedures would lead to re-growth after their collection and harvest, showed a spiritual connection to all life. This was their way of acting, and receiving a reaction.

Lucinda Fury

One Planet ♥ ♥ ♥ ♥ ♥ One People

HEALING IN A BEYOND SPACE

It seems as if there is an explosion of personal healings and transformations these days. Most of it is facilitated by the use of our minds and our hands. As a structural integrator practitioner, I'm in a constant state of awe at just how quickly the body adapts, incorporates change and heals itself; almost it seems, instantly. With our intuition as the flight plan and our heart as the navigator, we are able to send healing energy directly into human tissue.

My own experience with the power of the mind happened about ten years ago when in an awake state, still exhausted from a night of pain and interrupted sleep caused by my weak lower back. The pain had been fairly constant during the day, and I worried that I would become incapacitated or face surgery, or some other, equally horrible future. Nothing brings you down (in the dumps) like constant pain.

That evening I tried to get into a comfortable position and just got fifteen minute of restful sleep, I was playing a little film in my mind, of myself running on the beach and turning cartwheels like a child, totally free of pain and strong again. Then, to get a little further out of my body pain, I meditated on leaving this early plane and traveled out into the wonderful quiet of space. I saw my house get further away, and then I saw the whole earth below me - suddenly, I was out in space with planets and stars floating around me.

I was moving outwardly into space and saw a very bright spot. When I got closer, it was as an opening of light. I started into it, and felt I moved very fast and was suddenly in a place similar to a hospital. There on the table lay my spine. It was very huge bones, and a very phosphorus bright looking color. Just over the right kidney region were two little volcano shaped spots. Then a voice which I heard, yet seemed to come from me, spoke, "just move your hand over there", which I did. The volcanoes closed up, and I quickly awoke totally free of pain and feeling more refreshed and calm. I hadn't felt this way in years. I just sat in my chair for a time, and felt how good it was to sit and not have my back hurting.

I still don't know what happened, but it was real. I had touched my own power. I had a renewed faith that I would get well. I started searching for the way and Structural Integration was the answer for me. In this field, I am constantly amazed at the healing power of us all as demonstrated in Reiki, and other fields of healing using our energy, intent, and our hands.

The transformation that occurs from these health restoring modalities was expressed by (Emmett Hutchnis), "as the sensation of moving from weakness into strength and the exhilaration of owning a new part of oneself". That is exactly how I felt right after my dream vision, a sort of prophetic premonition of a cure for me. I had been allowed to "feel" this and become well again.

DuLois Lee

REIKI AND ROLE PLAYING

I heard about Reiki back in the mid-1980's when I lived in Los Angeles and hosted a TV cable show, "The Natural Psychic." One of my guests had studied Reiki and shared some of her experiences with me. I remember thinking they were amazing; healing of severe burns, distant healing, and so forth, and put it on my list of things "to do".

Not until I moved to Virginia Beach, and was guided by my inner voice to study Reiki did I follow through, and take Reiki I.

I have experienced Reiki with some wonderful people, and at one point in my life, two friends practically "force" me to lie on their table to receive the blessings of Reiki. I was so overwrought in my life that the energy they gave me felt like the recharging of my batteries. What a joy!

My friend told me about a client she had been working with, using Reiki, whose doctors could not diagnose the problem. The client had been in and out of the hospital, losing weight, and seemed potentially close to death, if the trend continued. He was depressed and seemed to have lost his will to live. She asked if I might go with her to the hospital, where he was on a heart monitor. His doctor was curious about the Reiki she had been giving him, and wanted to see how Reiki would react on the monitor. Would I help?

I was very intrigued by the possibility of a controlled test in a hospital setting under a doctor's sanction. Unfortunately, things did not work out exactly as planned. The machines were not working properly. The nursing staff had not been given written orders to allow our activities, and there was a lot of curiosity and suspicion on their part as they watched us with our hands on his chest. After about a half hour of rigmarole from the staff, trying out different monitors, using various adjustments, and coming and going repeatedly, I realized our uncontrolled 'test' was doomed.

Nevertheless, I felt it important to do a good healing, regardless of the scientific proof we were seeking. As my friend and I put our hands on the man, I began to talk with him quietly, as he had a semi-private room. I did not want to lose the attitude of protection he'd need for deeper emotional work.

I asked him how long he had been sick. He said several months. I asked him if anything unusual had happened just before he became ill. "Yes." I asked him if he would like to talk about it, using a gentle tone of voice.

"No, but I will". he began to tell the story of a woman he had loved very much, who just before he became ill had broken the relationship. I felt this was the 'red flag' of cause, I was seeking. After getting him to tell a little more about their relationship, I was given the guidance to use my psychic role-playing technique with him. (This technique is a hybridization of certain psycho-drama techniques, psychic reading skills, emotional release and visualization). My spiritual guides trained me in its development and it has been extremely useful in helping many of my clients.

Once clear on the direction I needed to go with this, I got to work. I told him I'd like to do some role-playing and that it was quite easy, that I just needed him to answer normally how he felt in response to what I would say. Meanwhile, my friend and I proceeded to give the initial Reiki. We felt this was soothing for him while I led the emotional release work.

I started the role of the estranged woman, but speaking from higher self attitude, loving, responsive, enlightened. (Every person has a higher self.) I acknowledged the man's hurt, anger and justification for feeling angry and disappointed. I gave space to all the held-in emotions I sensed he was carrying.

This gentleman visibly began to release tension and finally, tears as we continued to speak to one another. I encouraged him to say back to me in his own words how he felt as a result of being treated badly by her, saying I would not further antagonize or reject him, but really cared and was willing to understand his point of view. The man seemed amazed at this, but I held my ground, and repeated that his feelings were important and deserved to be validated. After we worked this angle for awhile, I sensed it was time to switch roles.

I suggested that now he be the woman (in his imagination), think and act like her. I would play the part of him. He seemed dubious, but I told him I'd start, and he was able to get into the swing of it. I became a strong advocate for the man, now verbally expressing deep hurt and rage which I psychically felt he was still carrying - and which I believed was toxifying his body. He visibly responded by a change of facial expressions, body relaxation movements, and more natural breathing as a result of his surrogate (I) expressing his hidden hurt and anger. It was as if an emotions lawyer had suddenly come to his defense and was winning his case! Perry Mason come to the rescue on a white horse - charge! The emotional energy in the room changed dramatically as we cleared more and more of the man's anger.

I did round three by taking back the role of the rejecting woman, and again took the point of view of higher self, responsive, sensitive and understanding. I expressed to this man who was again playing himself, how I heard his anger, respected it, and expressed that he was justified in feeling it. Relief became more and more evident in the man's demeanor. Within twenty or thirty minutes of this type of exchange, the blocked emotions surfaced, no longer toxifying this man's energy system, (I cannot prove that is what happened, but that is how it appeared to us).

Within 48 hours, he was released from the hospital, and began to immediately improve. Six months later, he is still doing fine. In fact, he has been out seeking a new relationship.

Linda Schiller

A STROKE IN TIME

It was a beautiful Monday morning in October - one of those Indian Summer days that make life such a joy, a morning that literally begs to be noticed. I was coming into the door of my office to make myself a cup of coffee and as I walked from the company kitchen, I found I could not grip the styrofoam cup. My right hand had lost all strength and there was a pain in my shoulder. At the time, I thought it was a pinched nerve and just tried to work it out through some movement. After about an hour, my right hand and arm felt weakened and sensationless. I figured something was wrong, and finally decided to go home from work.

My wife, a Reiki practitioner, started me on a Reiki treatment. We called Jeanne Gunn with whom I had taken my Reiki First and Second Degree and for whom I had great respect and trust. The two worked with me for four hours using their spiritual guidance and clairvoyant talents.

Right after this, the telephone rang and a dear friend and psychic minister called and stated "I think you need to go to the hospital to be checked out." Off we went to the closest hospital (Leigh Memorial). I went through the battery of tests, and was diagnosed as having had a mild stroke. I was referred back to another doctor, not on the hospital staff, who examined me using an echocardiogram. This also diagnosed any stroke. The doctor told me to take an aspirin a day, and he gave me some exercises to perform, using my arm and shoulder.

We organized a Reiki Team to provide me with treatment twice a week for the next four weeks. Friends, Reiki students and others gathered to offer their support and help. Others, unable to make it physically, prayed and visualized my recovery. Talk about energy coming in; talk about the strength of love; talk about realizing how good friendship felt!

After a few days of the Reiki treatments, the exercises, the aspirin, I went back to get re-examined. The doctor said he didn't know what it was I was doing, but whatever it was, I was healed and ready to go back to work.

My whole range of motion had returned, the pain was gone, and the stroke had left no clue as to its presence. It was indeed a miracle. Evidence of this was most strong as I noticed, felt, and experienced angels around me during my Reiki treatment. Their wings brushed against my body, and from that moment, not only was I healed, but I knew that I was healed beyond a doubt. The doctor's pronouncement only served to reinforce what I already knew, and served to provide me with renewed faith in the power available to us all, in my case delivered by angels. This experience opened my awareness in a way that is beyond mere knowing. This changed my life.

Lefty Hamblin

One Planet ♥ ♥ ♥ ♥ One People

I Count Myself as a . . .
RAINBOW WARRIOR

I was going to write about a time when I was very young and very small (3-4 years old), and I believed in angels. Then I thought, well, I will write about when I was (8-12 years old). When life seemed too much for me, I would go out into the woods and soothe away my cares, by becoming Snow White. It worked, I would sit very quiet and very still and the animals, (squirrels, chipmunks and one red fox) would go about their daily routine. I would softly cry my tears and gain my strength back. When I knew it was time to go home, I would leave this haven for another day.

I had no one to tell me that Mother Earth's strength was there, or about meditation. Maybe we were not thinking those things back in the old days!! Only a handful of enlightened peoples scattered around the world, would understand the crying out of a small child. Thank goodness for them. Then something happened. . . What??

Well, communications on earth became so advanced, we finally woke up to realize this planet is not really that big. We have started to wake up to the fact, that the people that live across the oceans are probably scared of wars, probably want to have freedom of religion, probably have the same thoughts that we do; isn't that amazing, they probably aren't the enemy!! What will the movies do when there isn't "A Bad Guy"??

Well, to stay on the subject. I was married young, and we raised three good children. They were honest and polite, with integrity and concern. We were very fortunate. We all worked together, helping each other, and were good neighbors, supporting our community and government. I think - no, I know - we thought this was the American Dream. We enjoyed working in the yard and around the house to make it look beautiful. We went without vacations and fancy clothes, but we worked together. We went to church. Still, there was something missing!! We got partially caught up in the American Myth - that life on this planet was about getting ahead, getting rich, cars in the driveway - material things.

The new myth - is the Rainbow Legend - the very personal soul development, the understanding of self, the knowing that life on our planet is really about waking up to Divine Source, our Creator. It is about waking up to treat where we live, how we live, and our neighbors with respect. We were well on track with behavior habits, but Change divided us, each one to find his own pathway and spiritual work on the planet.

Divorce is a word that became common place during the (70's, 80's and 90's). What happened to individuals has caused another great Change. Responsibilities for our actions seems to be someone else's. Dishonesty and greed for the dollar has caused the roaches to come out of the woodwork. Responsibility and commitment were lost, and the family unit dislocated. Look around today - turn on television and see killings, con-men schemes, drugs and addictions, abuse to children and women, incest, shootings on the highways, innocent victims, injustice after injustice. An awakened society can promote good from an awareness, of what we have become.

People have gathered in the USA to claim the American myth - getting all you can get, while the getting is good. We are all of the peoples from many nationalities, forgetting we are One, forgetting we are brothers and sisters, forgetting we form a united nation based on helping other nations. Many

One Planet ♥ ♥ ♥ ♥ ♥ One People

wanting to get something for nothing - the Change will come!!   But oh, are we really ready, for what we may bring upon us?? Do we realize, we are responsible for the Changes??

Mother Earth is hurting. The masses of people aren't working together. Honesty and integrity are forgotten words. However, there is a rise of spiritual growth - individuals searching, the explosion of awareness books on the market. Workshops facilitate role playing on any inner child hurts. Many are waking up, remembering from long ago - some need - some thought - something to jog the memory - the original myth!!

My waking up - was a need for answers to understand a divorce. What is your waking up??

An inner part of me was identifying with the hurts of Mother Earth. I kept thinking, "if I could just put my arms around the planet, around someone who is in pain, I could make it all better." That may have been my own inner pain. But, whatever, it lead me into taking Reiki - my first opportunity of acknowledged awareness, and of being on a pathway. Reiki helped me meditate, to hold close the sense of belonging, the inner guidance, the reawakening, to claim my spiritual rights. Reiki gave me strength for each day, no matter what was happening; getting me through the thoughts of suicide, through a divorce, through relationship endings, through losing everything. Now, people that know me, see an inner strength. An angel on my shoulder.

The many years of Reiki in my life, lead me through my angel death experience; my needing to be jogged big time. Books came that reawakened something in my cells, to remember the original instructions - intuition heightened - confirmations came.

My concern for the individual and for the planet; I realize is not a new concept to me. My concern with helping others make their connection and wake up is very important. Reading about the Rainbow Legend, the Medicine Wheel, the Circles of Life, the connection to Divine Source helped me realize my part in the Legend - more and more are awakening.

Much work is to be done. Our planet is hurting from the toxic wastes we have dumped onto and into her (gasoline, oils, fumes, garbage). If we think that our actions won't have a reaction we have our heads in the sand. The dolphins and whales have cried out by beaching themselves, the earth quakes from the drilling of holes in her body; weather patterns - have changed.

Yes, we can do something!!
Prayer: really deep committed prayer to help heal a certain portion of the earth (i.e. Rain Forests, waters, drugs, addictions, famine, plague, health, government agencies, injustices, peoples and nationalities who work against the whole). Prayer helped change the direction of a hurricane. United we stand, if we choose to.

Responsibility and Intention: Become aware of your personal attitude in driving, in your work habits and with co-workers, with your friends and community, with your nation and your lands. Remember the original instructions - the process of healing begins with us, our efforts and accomplishments, affect all future generations. The process begins with what is in our hearts.

Become a part of the Rainbow Legend - The original myth!!

S. Jeanne Gunn

One Planet ♥♥♥♥♥ One People

MIRACLE OF POWERLESSNESS

Miracles are strange, aren't they? I have begun to discover the true meaning of the power of healing. I have also glimpsed the meaning of death and illness, and they both have a purpose.

My experiences, with illness and death are not so new to me; they are old friends, as such can be, but I did not even know how important they both were until a short time ago. My near death experiences, my illnesses, the illnesses of friends and relatives have been the source of my education on human nature, healing and the importance of attitude in health maintenance.

From an early age, I have worked with the ill and the dying, including my own daughter, who died at the age of seven. My background in nursing has served me well. It was often frustrating when dealing with the terminally ill. The frustrations came both from the patient's attitudes and the attitudes of their families. Many, sadly, abandoned their loved ones at that glorious moment of transition from this plane to the next. It was not out of lack of love, but out of an inherent fear of death.

My own three death experiences have taught me a lot. The most vivid of them to this day is the experience in 1976 of my head going through the windshield of a car after being rear-ended. My experience of meeting three Spiritual Light Beings, one of gold, one of pink, and one of blue; in a warm, joyous place. I was told to come back to my body - to heal it and to live on. I remember that there was no pain until I returned to my broken body. Death has no pain; it's just a transition feeling. It seemed as if I could take whatever I wanted with me into death.

I sensed there was then a need for me to tell others nearing death of my experiences of lightness, airy feelings and joy to help them prepare for their own transitions. The staffs of nursing homes and hospitals treated death as an enemy to fight, inevitable as death is. Death was too often treated as abnormal, rather than as an ordinary, necessary and welcomed transition we all must experience.

Last summer, my husband's 86 year old aunt was in the hospital. She was in a coma in intensive care. My husband and I started talking to her and performing the simple motions of Reiki on her comatose body. We did this without a fear of death, but with the attitude of just helping the body with whatever it needed to ease whatever transition may be necessary, either into consciousness, or into death. Within three hours she was conscious and asking for a pen and paper. Through the weeks, she continued to improve; however, it was discovered during tests that she had cancer. On finding this out, her health deteriorated slowly. She slipped into a coma, then easily into death. The doctor was depressed, feeling a loss after such dramatic improvement. We explained it was her choice to go,

My nursing experience includes many years of holistic health. Reiki was a natural next step for me, and I knew it when I had first heard of it. Healing through Reiki involves attitude. It seems to relieve the pain of disease. Reiki seems to open the universal mind from the macro to the molecular levels within ourselves. With Reiki, there is a doorway to an energy source; a conduit to spiritual forces beyond our understanding. Healing is acknowledging the ability of own bodies to unite forces with mind and spirit.

We also need to realize that there is in each life a time when that person's work is done and it is time to leave; but, instead of just going over into the next realm, we seem to need to create illness and disease to give ourselves permission to leave. Again, it is the feeling of powerlessness that we are trying to fight, and that is when the most power comes through, as we need it, as it is appropriate. Guilt, anger and fear too often feed the disease. If we can work on these feelings, we can also diminish the effects of the disease.

In doing Reiki treatments, sometimes the client's feelings are brought to the forefront, allowing them to address the issues underlying the disease. This often leads to crying, sorrow, and the feelings of powerlessness and fear. In the channeling of Reiki energy, a way is opened for the communion between the client and spirit to form a bond of healing. It is to encourage good attitudes and positive acknowledgments of the powerlessness of human beings in the spiritual realms, and their ability to tap into those divine powers with little else than faith and release of feelings.

Sheila Hamblin

MASTERFUL CONSCIOUSNESS

What came to pass one sleepless night was an out-of-the-ordinary inner event which would eventually repeat itself.

After walking circles through rooms and doorways late one night, I received a strong impression that it was time to sit down. In doing so my whole being gracefully slipped into a very interesting, different reality. Before long a determined message made itself known. The feeling of the message revolved around the idea that at this point in time I had outgrown my name, Helen. The unexpected sense was saying the vibration of the letters and their placement in my name no longer served me. Almost instantly a void, like a hollow pipe, placed itself over my head and sucked my birth name identity right out of my skull. Zap, my name was gone.

A small remnant of understanding was left in its place. It brought these thoughts to my mind. Why be so surprised? Change and evolution are natural in our universe. Everything always moves on in spite of itself. I found the whole idea rather intriguing. I thought how interesting it would be if in our society we really did change our name at certain points in our personal growth, making our name fit our newly evolved state of mind.

In a flash a ball of energy seemed to explode down the pipe and I had a new name. But a split second before the flash happened I recall saying to myself, "So this is what it feels like to be a man without a country." In that second I felt so alone and lost.

Here I sat in the middle of the night with a new name - BABALUSKA. There it was! What was it? No understanding, no reasoning, no logic came with the experience. Nothing.

In the following months my friends and co-workers began calling me by my new name. But it wasn't long before my familiar birth name came back. Babaluska was pushed into the background but never completely out of the picture. The event was never forgotten.

This particular cosmic-like experience of "lifting" surfaced a second time. I only thought about these two experiences when asked to write material for this book. I suspect my intuition pointed me toward these experiences because they are similar and because the second one related to my being a Reiki Master.

I want to preface the second experience with a few Reiki facts. In 1980 1 was the first Reiki Master in Wisconsin. This was at a time when the Reiki Mastership was held in very high esteem, and in my case it contributed to a quantum leap in transforming my consciousness. In those years the third degree was considered a major commitment, both personally and financially, truly a giant step into mastery.

The second "lifting" happened after years of teaching and being the practitioner in hundreds of treat- treatments. The word healing was lifted out. The lifting action took with it my learned assumptions tied to the word healing - the idea that illness is bad, there's something to get rid of, or even something to fear. Society functions on these assumptions, as do healers. The attachments, assumptions, and judgments tied to the word healing were released.

Little did I know how important this release was for my future growth. At the time I could see no real reason for or any particular advantage to my newly arranged consciousness. I now see that everything including illness or any discomfort can be viewed from the new perspective of natural change, ongoingness, and evolution. Looking at discomfort primarily as an experience of evolution, is evidence of forming a masterful consciousness.

We often read about extremely open minded people who have gleaned great benefit from what society calls "illness" or "handicap," especially when a major shift in consciousness happens. Even if no physical cure takes place these individuals still end up with a highly elevated state of well-being.

I am one of those individuals society views as handicapped. You see, I came into this life without a leg. I've spent 61 years wearing a prosthesis. This particular condition has proved to be a catalyst through which I have had one personal transformation after another. Then 9 years ago a monumental 'proclamation message' propelled me into a full time search. The message announced I would and could manifest a leg where one is missing.

Needless to say, the possibility idea threw me into major shock. After all, I was part of society's traditional thinking and the idea of growing a leg never entered by mind. In the years that followed scores of new ideas started to override my old, lack picture and I began a re-education process unlike anything imaginable. I write about it in detail in my book called *Silent Mind Speaks*. First I rearranged my thinking patterns to include the leg manifestation concept with all its ramifications and then researched the kind of consciousness it would take to actually make possible such an accomplishment. I did not see the absence of a leg as bad, needing to be fixed, nor did the circumstance leave me fearful of life. The absence led me to a transforming process having nothing to do with any of the traditional forms of healing. The "liftings" allowed me to move beyond personal identities and patterns from any learned practice or modality. I was allowed to focus wholeheartedly on the true universal energy behind all the ideas.

This is where I am today. I'm discovering the ins and outs of a lifestyle which has its primary focus on transforming the whole self and allowing the creation of a leg to be a by-product. I began re-teaching myself with what I call quantum ideas. The difficult part was to imagine what it is like to believe in something other than what my eyes see. My physical eyes tell me something is missing but the eye of my greater self says I will see it when I believe it. I know now why I must place my attention on "growing" all of me, not just a leg. It becomes increasingly clear to me that growing an inclusive, unlimited, infinite consciousness comes first and foremost. Then anything is possible.

The concept I call evenness became part of this journey. My self-teaching of evenness meant being perfectly OK with wearing a prosthesis the rest of my life and being equally OK with creating a leg. I understand having too much thought energy wrapped up in a particular outcome is a block to an actual desire. To me evenness means not to lean too heavily toward one side or the other, but to keep both in balance, creating a stage upon which I can act out endless possibilities.

Adding to the evenness concept another turning point came when I owned the fact that I always was, am now, and will always be an infinite being. I no longer need to search for it. I accept I as an original, natural energy which is in constant flow. My thoughts now go beyond the idea of healing into consciously and deliberately aligning with the inherent flow of life.

Each day my consciousness expands. Each day I am prepared for the uncommon and the unexpected. Each day the supreme intelligence of the "ultimate prodigy" is at work. Onward into masterful consciousness.

Helen Borth

About Human Energy
An Interview with Larry

Larry: Knowledge about our human energy fields is of great importance to our total well-being. What has been know in the past needs to be updated to fit with the present time.

Question: What is the first thing you want to say about energy?

Larry: A person's energy field is immediately around them, probably 3 to 4 feet around, above, and below. I believe this is the area of the workable field.

Question: Do you mean around and Through the person?

Larry: The field emanates from the very deepest core of an individual. It emanates through the molecular level of the body from the part of us we have yet to discover, the true source, the true being. Energy/matter is not only color. It is sound, movement, waves, and in every moment different. All of these aspects 'speck' to me when I'm in a session with another person.

Question: Do objects give off this emanation?

Larry: Yes! The chair in the corner, the table over there gives off a field of energy. It's energy is more passive. It still has motion/movement and is changing but it doesn't give off the vibrant colors that humans or animal do. A child's energy is a little more dimensional and as a child develops the hues, colors, shapes and sound unfolds.

Question: Are you constantly aware of this energy?

Larry: Yes. It's been with me since birth, or at least as long as I can remember. I have had to learn to control the seeing and hearing of the fields.

Question: When you look at a person from one day to the next do you notice changes in their fields?

Larry: It changes from one moment to the next. It's like a kaleidoscope of colors and sound. With every thought we think, story or song we hear, the field changes.

Question: Can you sense the difference between someone who has no awareness of his/her own field and someone who has a rather good awareness of the field and the thought relationship to it?

Larry: Definitely. An individual who is really <u>unaware</u> has a 'yo-yo' acting field. The energy changes intensely from small to large, from brilliant to dark. On the other hand, a person who's <u>aware</u> of his/her space and presence doesn't flux in the same manner. Their field changes but it's more subtle and the emanation of the field is more in control of it, rather than the field being in control of them.

Question: How can we recognize if we're the kind of person who might have a 'yo-yo' type energy?

Larry: A good indicator if energy controls you, is if you get tired easily and for no apparent reason and/or have emotional swings. Physical manifestations such as tension and stress can act as indicators.

Question: Do you experience peoples' energies through your senses or through your sight?

Larry: I do both. I often hear people say they wish they could see the energy. That would be fine, but I think it is more beneficial to develop a sense of it; that gut level feeling. There is so much to see everywhere you look in the energy world it gets confusing. Even overwhelming. So much of it isn't necessary to observe. The endless clouds of human thought everywhere, look like static or snow on TV.

Getting a sense on a gut level that things are not just right and knowing how to change them; to me is actually more trustworthy. I have taught myself ways to go through the confusion. You see, energy is everywhere. No matter where you go you step into energy.

Your place of work is full of energy. It's field is made up of energy from the people who are present, the remnants of people who were there in the past and the beginning of the formation of energy from the people who will arrive today.

Our energy arrives before our body. What is important is how we deal with all these flows of energy which determines if we play victim or master, 'yo-yo' or stable. A master knows energy can be rearranged and it moves according to thought. By knowing he is in charge he can uplift the entire field if that appears to be necessary.

Question: What else is important to know about energy?

Larry: I am finding that many past concepts in the field of energy are becoming obsolete. In the past we broke down the energy field or aura into small divisions, giving them human characteristics and psychological definitions. This was a good attempt at making our conscious mind comfortable with the unknown and gave us a way to rationalize and place blame for our behavior.

We no longer have the time to analyze and separate ourselves from our aura in this manner. The physical body along with its energy field is one indivisible unit! Whole, complete within itself and when worked with in this manner one soon realizes, the whole is greater than the sum of its parts.

Past ideas of wearing special objects or using colors to improve an individual's energy no longer are creating their desired effect. Because, as I, and as well as many other energy practitioners, have come to know there is nothing more powerful as *thought* to permanently change the human energy field.

Energy also works on sympathetic vibrations. If you go to a music store with a wall full of guitars and violins and you play a note on one of those instruments, you can hear all the remaining instruments on the wall vibrate or 'sing'.'. Likewise, if you become overly concerned with someone's illness, you help that illness to become stronger by emanating a vibration that's on the same wave-length. But, if you broadcast an energy field that's full of life and energy, you'll help those vibrations in another person to come forth or 'sing'.'.

The concept of energy coming from several major points in the body, I also believe, is out-dated. Each atom in our body emanates and creates our energy field. When you combine the emanation of all the atoms, molecules and cells, that is where our energy emanates from. Our field or aura many believe to be egg-shaped or oval in nature. That may have been true at one time, but I believe that collectively as a human race our energy has evolved into a circular or spherical presentation.

Like the atom, we have a nucleus, or body, and orbiting electrons that create the outer 'shell' of our aura; and the one thing that dramatically affects our field or aura is *inharmonious thoughts* about ourselves and life in general. These thoughts do all kinds of crazy things to the field, like making it look like an amoeba, rather than a vibrant force.

Question: Would you suggest a practice which we could use to help ourselves?

Larry: When someone's field ends up looking like an amoeba, which in most cases causes pain or discomfort in the body, I recommend two methods to reclaim and restore the aura's natural charge.

First - find a yard-stick and holding it from one end with your out-stretched arm draw arcs in the air. Draw them from side to side, above your head, down in front of you to develop a sense of the approximate size and shape the energy field should be. Spend some time following the end of that stick. Memorize the sense of space and the size of the field - for definition. Visualize that same space behind you and below your feet, down through the floor. Affirm to yourself that "this entire space is me, this is what I have to offer and this is what I bring to every moment of my life".

Second - I recommend to many of my clients that they spend some time every day moving their own energy. No one can do it better! No one really has the right to move your energy but you, yourself. So, keeping the edge of the aura in mind, that the first exercise defined, pull from your upper body, in straight lines, energy to meet that edge. Do your pulling in all directions remembering to use straight lines. The goal is to create a *star-burst* emanation centralized in the *heart* area.

Question: Give us a closing statement.

Larry: Here are some ideas for those interest in the world of energy.

First, keep in mind that only about .01% of our total being is the physical body. So, with 99.99% of us intangible, unseen and waiting to be discovered, isn't this where most of our attention needs to be placed?

Second, energy does not work on any rules or regulations we humans can understand. As a Master Reiki teacher, I recommend that when working with energy, you 'make it up as you go'. Trust your heart, inner guidance and your own creativity and don't bring formats, formulas or pre-conceived ideas to any situation while working with energy.

Ultimately, energy is not about healing or finding the perfect mate or even changing the world. Energy is about discovering our own true nature, evolving and developing our own sense of unity or oneness with the universe.

Larry Borth

A Quantum Outlook

A centered existence is marked by the interconnectedness of mind and body. Evidence proving that the one can, and does, influence the other is growing. Enough non-medical healings have taken place to allow us to consider abandoning the label of chance applied to them. There is a substantial case history of *quantum* healing, wherein conscious, purposeful, directed thought can be applied through the brain to cause physical healing.

However, we're not concerned with numbers. Significance lies not in numbers but in remembering - *these healings were the opposite of chance; they were not accidental remissions.* These *quantum* healings occurred *only after* a decision had been made to reverse disease and *to heal.*

The subjects accepted the presence of the invasive disease in their bodies, but absolutely refused to accept its inevitable devastation. They in effect said, "I know you're there but I refuse to submit to your indignity." That *quantum* step, moving up radically to a higher level of accepting the relation between one's mind and body, was the beginning of the cure in each case.

The ability to embrace such a belief - and it *is* a belief, not a laboratory-proven medical technique - and understandably is not popular with the medical profession. Doctors in most medical fields are not committed to simple healing; they are committed to healing through medicine. Consider the shambles in the medical field were the belief in *quantum* healing to be universally accepted as the basis for healing.

It's interesting to conjecture how many doctors in any field of expertise would stand aside as medical-experts in the face of such a *quantum* healing and be willing to submit themselves along with the patient to the conviction that the *healing* was the overpowering consideration, and not how it was brought about. I dare say very few at this point could resist the urge either subtly or overtly to nudge the patient back into the channel carved by traditional use of medicine.

That Dr. Deepak Chopra's book, *Quantum Healing, Exploring the Frontiers of Mind/Body Medicine,* is a national bestseller simply reflects national interest in this expanding field. Dr. Chopra is not a pie-in-the-sky theorist but a practicing endocrinologist, and thus able to describe authoritatively the latest experiments illustrating chemical reactions in the body produced by the brain, i.e., by a thought pattern. Nor is he by any means alone in this work. Nationally recognized and respected scientists like the renowned Dr. Edelman are working to determine where thought begins in the brain.

It is not a great step anymore from brain to body, as evidenced by what is being learned from high-tech electro-photography of brain cells' actual functions and corresponding cell responses elsewhere in the body. Since choice is given to all, the choice to accept or reject the limitless benefits of *quantum* healing could mean the difference between life and death. What is there to lose?

Marius Broekhuizen

One Planet ♥ ♥ ♥ ♥ ♥ One People

GLOSSARY

Alveoli - Tiny sacks which actually deposit the air we breathe into the blood vessels, tiny pouches shaped like grapes.

Astral - Refers to the energy/matter frequency band just beyond the etheric. The astral body is strongly affected by emotion. The plane in which we dream, the body of the fourth chakra.

Aura - The electro-magnetic field surrounding life forms; the soul's light force as it manifests through the body; the extended energy around the human body which alters in radiance and color depending upon the state of physical, mental, emotional and spiritual health.

Catarrh - Inflammation of the mucous membrane.

Celestial Plane - The realm of light, visualization, and archetype; the body of the sixth chakra.

Chakra - (Sanskrit) Wheel of light. One of the energy centers within the body, the spinning of which generates an electro-magnetic or auric field around the body; associated with various states of evolution, consciousness, physical organs, glands, colors and stones.

Channeling - A term used to describe the healing technique in which one person (the healer) acts as a channel to transfer various frequencies of energy to another person (the client) for the purpose of rebalancing chakras; thereby facilitating stress

Clairvoyance - The ability to perceive matters or images beyond the range of normal perception, including subtle body energies, chakras, and auric fields

Crystals - Nature's three-dimensional geometric forms whose outward appearance mirrors the internalized perfect ordering of atoms. Crystals are capable of reflecting pure light and color that can be channeled in numerous ways.

Electromagnetic Field - The space around a charged object where an electric field exists in a perpendicular direction to a magnetic field.

Energy - (ancient Egyptian) primeval spirit of the universe; fundamental life force, an innate law from the beginning of creation that makes all particles comprehend, vibrate at different speeds; (Eastern Indian) a limited manifestation of the Almighty as the changeless aspect of the One; energy is magnetism, found everywhere moving throughout all the universe in every direction.

Etheric Plane - Realm of pure sound and pure thought void of light; the spiritual template for the physical world, the body of the fifth chakra.

Great Central Sun - The omnipotent eternal source of light existing in the center of the infinite universe out of which radiates the entire panoramic creation: the power that creates the infinite universe.

Higher Consciousness - Attuned and aligned with the source of power and truth with the Self; the neutral aspect of awareness that identifies with spiritual light and is fulfilled by creatively manifesting that light through thoughts, feelings, words and actions.

Ketheric Plane - Realm of pure energy and spirit and emergence with Deity, the body of the seventh chakra.

Kirlian Photography - A method of capturing on a photographic plate an image of what is purported to be an aura energy that emanates from animals and plants and that undergoes changes in accordance with physiological or emotional changes.

Kundalini - The awakened or sleeping "serpent power" located in the first chakra.

Lazer - A device which produces coherent light; directed to stimulate particular accupoints for relief of illness.

Laying on of Hands - A general term for a type of direct, hands on type of healing, sometimes referred to as psychic healing or magnetic healing, i.e. Reiki.

Left Brain - Refers to the left cerebral hemisphere, which operates in analytical, logical, and linear modes of thought.

Medicine Wheel - (Native American) a wheel that depicts the total universe, and the sacred way that all Creation balances; a tool to gain wisdom, guidance and growth from external clues; the wheel teaches gentle dealing and respect for nature, its creatures and people; teaches one to sing the song of the world, to become whole people and one with the universe, wheel tells of the responsibilities of all to "return" good to Earth Mother in order to keep her balanced and prevent her from becoming sick (earthquakes, wars, floods, hurricanes).

Oversoul - Those who exist in the etheric planes and are aligned and attuned to the source of spiritual light; those serving non-physical spiritual guides, in the evolutionary process of individuals and of the planet; advanced beings who originally inhabited the earth and seeded the root races; those forming the brotherhood of light.

Peristalsis - Rhythmic involuntary contractions of the muscle fibers of the intestinal canal whereby the contents are mixed with the digestive juices and forced along the canal.

Prana - Also known as (chi) or (ki). The name given to the vital life force or energy in the body.

Quantum Physics - The branch of physics which studies the energetic characteristics of matter at the subatomic level.

Right Brain - The right cerebral hemisphere, associated with spatial, intuitive, artistic, symbolic, and non-linear thought.

Scanning - A healing technique in which the healer moves his or her hand over the edges of the client's aura field in an attempt to obtain necessary information about the energy flow.

Second Sight - The capacity to see auras, chakras, energy fields, as well as remote, past or future objects or events.

Soul - The spark of infinite spirit existing within each individual; that which holds the key to ultimate truth and power, the unique personalized aspect of the cosmic force.

Spirit - The omnipresent intelligent life force comprising and creating all manifest and non-manifest states of reality; the cosmic force which is eternally existent, changeless and true, the common denominator throughout the entire creation, the spark of life, the light, the truth and the source of all that is.

Star Children - Those beings incarnated on the earth that originate from other planets and/or galaxies; those lightworkers who have come to teach the higher laws and principles of the universe.

Subconscious - That part of the personality which dwells below the surface of waking consciousness and controls automatic human functions. It subliminally records all information taken in by the senses and is conditioned, programmed by rewards, punishments, and messages that subtly build up our internal picture of self worthiness.

Superconsciousness - That part of the higher soul structure which is usually unconscious but accessible to the personality. The superconscious contains higher wisdom, whereas the subconscious relates with the personality of a six year old child.

Thought Forms - A manifestation of a strong thought or emotion as an actual energetic structure within an individual's auric field.

Thymus Gland - An important gland, nourished by the heart chakra, which helps to regulate the immune response.

Thyroid Gland - A small butterfly shaped gland in the neck region which produces thyroxin, a hormone that regulates the body's metabolic rate.

Vibrations - The periodic motion of a body or wave in alternating opposite directions from the position of zero when equilibrium has been disturbed.

Vision Quest - An essential part of a young Native American's initiation into adulthood. The youth is sent on a vigil involving fasting and praying in order to gain some sign of the presence and nature of his guardian spirit. Often the sign is a dream in which his guardian spirit appears to him, usually in animal form, instructs him, and takes him on a visionary journey.

BIBLIOGRAPHY

A.C.T.A. Quarterly: Spring 1993

Arnold, L. & Nevius, S. The Reiki Handbook. Harrisburg, PA: PSI Press, 1982

Baginski, B. & Sharamon, S. Universal Life Energy. Mendocino, CA: Life Rhythm Publ., 1985.

Bletzer, June G. Donning Encylopedic Psychic Dictionary. Norfolk, VA: Donning Publ., 1986.

Brennen, B. Hands of Light. New York: Batam Books, 1988.

Bruyere, Rosalyn L . Wheels of Light. New York, NY: Simon & Schuster, 1989.

Carter, Albert E. The Miracles of Rebound Exercise.

Chopra, Dr. Deepak Ageless Body, Timeless Mind. New York, NY: Harmony Books, 1993.

Chopra, Dr. Deepak Quantum Healing. New York, NY: Bantum Books, 1989.

Gerber, R. Vibrational Medicine. Santa Fe, NM: Bear & Co., 1988.

One Planet ♥ ♥ ♥ ♥ ♥ One People

Haberly, H. Reiki: Hawayo Takata's Story. Garett Park, MD: Archedigm Publ., 1990.

Hall, Manly P. The Secret Teachings of All Ages. Los Angles, CA:
     The Philosophical Research Society, 1988.

Hay, Louise L. You Can Heal Your Life. Santa Monica, CA: Hay House, Inc., 1984.

Jensen, Dr. Bernard Doctor-Patient Handbook. Escondido, CA: Bernard Jensen Enterprises, 1976.

Newsletter: Healing Crisis. Harper, TX: Well Being Ranch, 1990.

Newsletter: Rainbow Ray Focus. Magnificent Consummation, Inc. Sedona, AZ: 83339

Null, Gary Body Mind Spirit Magazine. Book Listings: 1-800-441-5569

Pierrakos, John C. Core Energetics. Mendocino, CA: Life Rhythm Publ., 1990.

Rand, William L. Reiki, The Healing Touch. Southfield, MI: Vision Publ., 1991.

Raphaell, Katrina Crystal Healing. Santa Fe, NM: Aurora Press, 1987.

Russell, Walter The Electric Nature of the Universe. Waynesboro, VA:
     University of Science and Philosophy, 1991.

Schulman, Martin Karmic Astrology. Vol. I York Beach, ME: Samuel Weiser, Inc., 1975.

Sherwood, Keith Chakra Theraphy. St. Paul, MN: llewellyn Publ., 1993.

The Family Ark, % Womark, P.O. Box 279, Rollingyford, NH 03869

Vannini, Vanio & Giuliano Pagliani The Color Atlas of Human Anatomy. New York, NY:
     Harmony Books, 1979.

Walker, James R. Lakota Belief and Ritual. Lincoln, NE: University of Nebraska Press, 1980.

Walker, Norman W. Colon Health: The Key to a Vibrant Life. Presscot, AZ: Norwalk Press, 1979.

Wolfe, Amber In The Shadow of the Shaman. St. Paul, MN: Llewellyn Publ., 1988.

Zehr, Dr. Albert Healthy Steps. Abundant Publ., 1990. Address: P.O. Box 250, 7101C-12th St.
     Delta, BC V4E 2A0.

NETWORKING SOURCES

(This publisher is not responsible for any address or telephone changes)

AUTHOR: S. Jeanne Gunn, P,O. Box 1734, Virginia Beach, VA 23451
        Quantum Reiki Master, Bodywork Massage Therapist
        Workshops on Reiki 1, 2, Quantum, 3, Will Travel for Workshops
        Founder and Editor: Reiki and Beyond Training Center and Newsletter
        Angelic Counseling, Artist - Wind Dancer

Borth, Helen   Wauwatosa, Wisconsin
        Director and Co-founder of Institute of Self Awareness, Reiki Master
        Instructor and Developed: Quantum Awareness (Home Study Course) 12-90 min tapes
        Author: "Silent Mind Speaks"   (414) 463-5731

Borth, Larry   Co-founder of Institute of Awareness
        Auric Energy Specialist. Private Sessions or Will Travel for Workshops
        Reiki Master, Produced: "About Human Energy" - (audio cassette)   (414) 463-5731

Broekhuizen, Marius   Ossipee, New Hampshire
        Writer, Novel: "Islands" being released in 1994
        Teacher, Lecturer: Creative Writing, Will Travel
        Business: Scriptech Communication Design (editing)   (603) 539-2920

Cunningham, Daniel   Virginia Beach Virginia
        Firewalk Instructor, Edgar Cayce Foundation member and employee
        Masters in Library Science, Peace Corp (3 yrs) Massage Health Care
        Reiki, Working on Book "Walking on Fire"

Essig, Joan   Virginia Beach Virginia
        Teacher: Reilly School of Massotheraphy (A.R.E.), Massage Therapist
        Nurse, Energy Worker, Reiki, Background Atlantean Culture
        Past Life Counseling, Will Travel and Teach   (804) 437-9631

Foster, Pandora   Washington DC
        Business: Pandora's Box: (Word Processing- resumes, legal documents, proposals, reports, etc.)
        Desktop Publishing: (brochures, business cards, flyers, pamphets, etc.)
        Poet, Songwriter, Reiki   Business (202) 232-4825

Fury, Lucinda (Lumis) Virginia Beach Virginia
        Writer: Poetry, Childrens Book "The Learning of Nimwanaya" - Release Date 1994
        Lecturer for children on Native American Culture and Beliefs
        Artist: Native American Ceremonial Art - Reiki   Office (804) 468-9989

Gunn, Jennifer   Vineland New Jersey
        Nurse - Emergency Room, Volunteer Rescue Squad - 7 years
        Exchange Student - Denmark, Firewalker - Reiki

Haidle, Jim & Jill Wolf (Oak, Ash & Thorn Co.) Norfolk, Virginia
     Electronic and Computer Background and Designer
     Promotional Materials: (newsletters, business cards, greeting cards, etc.)
     Reiki, (Future Books - Science Fiction & Pagan Cookbook)   (804) 480-0760

Hamblin, Sheila and Lefty   Norfolk Virginia
     Directors: Circles of the Sacred Earth (Medicine Wheel) monthly meetings
     Workshops: Shaman, Rattle, Crystal, Chakras, Medicine Shields
     Reiki Healing Work - Intuitive Clairvoyant Readings   (804) 855-9907

Hutton, Ruth   Virginia Beach Virginia
     Cardiology Nurse, Reiki and Energy Work   (804) 481-3245

Jones, Katherline Teelee   Virginia Beach Virginia
     Author: "Angels Whisper", Published 1988
     Gardening, Course of Miracles - Reiki   (804) 496-3440

Kuehling, Joseph Chesapeake, Virginia
     Mystic Arts: Tarot Master, Qabalistic, Celtic (1967) Reiki (1985) Prana
     Integration (1985) Zen Training (1967--) Egyptian Esoterisist
     Teacher: Tarot, Healing, Dreams at Institute for Spiritual Development, WDC
     Writing Book on Shamanism, Qabala, Egypt & Metaphysics   (804) 548-3765

Larson, Lucille   Northfield New Jersey
     Writer: Articles and Poetry for local Newsletters
     World Traveler, Silva - Reiki

Lee, DuLois   Virginia Beach Virginia
     Structural Integration Therapist, C.M.T.
     Real Estate Brokerage   (804) 578-9607

Permel, Ramone   Virginia Beach Virginia
     Free Lance Photographer: Weddings, Bar Mitzvah's, Family Group, Children
     Commercial Photography, Specializing in Creative Black and White photo's
     Travels - East Coast area   Office (804) 855-2726

Rine, Debbie   Virginia Beach Virginia
     Teacher: Psychic Development Classes, Medicine Wheel - Reiki
     Newsletter: Rine News   Intuitive Clairvoyant Counseling   (804) 474-0080

Schiller, Linda   Virginia Beach Virginia
     Teacher: Lightworker Intensive (Psychic Development Class) Will Travel
     Newsletter: Two Suns (earth changes)
     Intuitive Clairvoyant Counseling   (804) 363-8445

Spears, Terri   Virginia Beach Virginia
     Writer and Lecturer, Will Travel
     Spiritual Counselor - Health and Life Readings, C.M.T.   (804) 428-1138

Story, Dr. Stephanie   Heritage Center, Virginia Beach Virginia
     Doctor of Naturopathic Medicine, Homeopathy, Herbal Medicine
     Worked in WDC for 10 years on Environmental Issues
     Nutritional and Lifestyle Counseling   Office   (804) 428-7979

One Planet ♥ ♥ ♥ ♥ ♥ One People

Stone, Brenda   Virginia Beach Virginia
        Visionary, Crystal Readings - Reiki

Whitehill, Archie   Norfolk Virginia
        Writer: Various Newsletters on Holistic and Psychic Topics, Working on Book
        Business: Quest, Inc. (Career Development Services)
        Internet Address: archie @ infi.net or   (804) 627-4620

Zieman, Claire   Virginia Beach Virginia
        Co-founder: Imagine Perfect Health - Holistic Retreat
        Colon Hydrotherapist - Nutritional Counselor   Office (804) 422-2458

Reiki Alliance
P. O. Box 41
Cataldo, ID 83810-1041   Tele: (208) 682-3535

Reiki and Beyond Training Center
P. O. Box 1734
Virginia Beach, VA 23451   Tele: (804) 422-0087

Reiki Outreach International
P.O. Box 55008
 Santa Clarita CA 91385 USA   Tele: (805) 259-1393

Specialty School for Quantum Thinking
Institute of Self Awareness, Inc.
P.O. Box 26005
Wauwatosa, WI 53226   Tele: (414) 527-1160

Institute of Self Awareness, Inc.　　　P.O. Box 26005 Wauwatosa, WI 53226　　　414-527-1160

SPECIALTY
SCHOOL *for* Quantum Thinking

<u>New Field of Study</u> - *a brilliant synthesis of science, sociology, philosophy, psychology, and spirituality which together act as an exceptional guide to personal transformation.*

Free rental program!!!
Unbelievable Bargain - Act Now

- **"*Quantum Awareness*" home study course**

  Developed and instructed by Helen Borth

  Call **414-527-1160** and ask for the tape set contract. When the contract is returned you will receive twelve 90 minute live class recordings plus *The Morning Before* lesson book.

  Here is an unique opportunity to participate in class dynamics while sitting at home in your favorite chair.

  The course is courageous, freeing, and personally strengthening through its 4 transformational learnings:

  - How to use the principles of thought and the power of mind
  - How to see yourself and your place in the universe from a quantum perspective
  - How connectedness applies to the mind/body relationship and the universe as a whole
  - How **Visioning** is the means to becoming a quantum person.

  (You will be charged for shipping and handling)

- Book - *"Silent Mind Speaks"* by Helen Borth
  Using the unbelievable messages given her in the last 9 years Helen's story tells how she was able to courageously take her handicap into a truly amazing personal transformation.
  Cost $8.00　　　S&H $2.00

- Tape -" *About Human Energy*"
  By Larry Borth....*Auric Energy Specialist/Reiki Master*
  An outstanding tape of energy information valuable to everyone especially those drawn to Reiki. The included perspectives illustrate what it means to move beyond Reiki.
  Cost $8.00　　　S&H $2.00

One Planet ♥♥♥♥♥ One People

One Planet ♥ One People

Reiki and Beyond Training Center
non-profit organization
P. O. Box 1734
Virginia Beach, Virginia 23451
Telephone: (804)422-0087 or 800-892-0017

REIKI AND BEYOND TRAINING CENTER

Our Center's Reiki concept and how it work . . .

It is our desire to help guide the individual onto the pathway of their choice using the Reiki Life Force Energy. Reiki is not just for hands-on healing, "Reiki is a way of life". Whatever your career - whatever your way of life - *the endless source of Divine God energy is available.*

♥   Reiki helps you to go within for Meditation and Prayer

♥   Reiki is using your experiences and working with others: sharing

♥   Reiki is a personal Attunement and Initiation

♥   Reiki is a personal Purification of the Soul

♥   Reiki is a method of tapping into the Divine Source of Energy

♥   Reiki is Service: to Yourself, to the Brotherhood of Man, to the Planet

♥   Reiki is a Beginning: into Evolvement and your Right of Passage

♥   Reiki is what Jesus and the other Masters conveyed with their service to Mankind

♥   Reiki was re-discovered from long ago and is ever evolving into the Beyond

♥   Reiki Alignment connects you with your Spiritual Guides and Angelic Ones

♥   Reiki does not interfere with any religious preference or background

We want to help you journey towards understanding yourself and understanding the energy fields surrounding all living things. We will guide you with your personal attunement/initiation connection, thereby enabling you to find the many secrets of life and your right of passage. From there, you have the opportunity to take this information out into the world. You will be healing yourself, and those around you by the presence of your energy.

Become the *Wind Dancer* in your dance of life.
Join us for a training session, or sponsor a training session in your area.

One Planet ♥ ♥ ♥ ♥ ♥ One People

Reiki & Beyond I and II

Reiki I and Reiki II are taught together in a two day seminar or week-end intensive. The following are those techniques which will be covered and are available in the Reiki and Beyond Healing Manual.

- History
- What Is Reiki and Using Reiki
- Energy Fields and Chakra System
- Giving a Treatment (Hand Positions)
- Scanning and Beaming
- Letting Go and Empowering Goals
- Reiki Symbols: Power, Emotional & Mental, Distant Healing
- Your Personal Attunement and Initiation into Reiki
- Symbol: 10 Levels of Awareness and Attunement
- Meditation
- Crystal Ceremony and Ritual (Native American)

Reiki and Beyond - Quantum Level

A One day intensive guiding and strengthening you in <u>advanced techniques</u>. Information is available in the Reiki and Beyond Healing Manual.

- Reiki Meditation
- Reiki Usui Master Symbol
- Reiki Psychic and Lazer Techniques
- Body Awareness and Nutrition
- Technique: Lifetime Ray and Color Energy
- Golden Light Body Alignment: Symbols and Attunement
- Golden Light Body Alignment: Procedure for Initiation
- Beyond Experiences - (how they work for you)

Perquisite: Reiki Quantum Level is required before taking Reiki III/Masters.

Reiki III/Masters

Reiki Master Class teaches you: how to attune and initiate others into Reiki. This is a two day intensive. Recommendation: Reiki Quantum Level and Reiki III are taught together as a three day intensive. Masters Class includes the following:

- Reiki I and II: Procedure for Attunement
- Tibetan Healing Method: Symbols & Procedure for Attunement
- Reiki III: Procedure for Attunement
- Reiki Meditation - Going Beyond
- Mysteries: Personal Evolvement and Commitment
- Practice Time
- Crystal Ceremony & Ritual (Native American)
- Teachers Manual provided

Reiki and Beyond Training

Reiki and Beyond I and II:

This class is taught together during a week-end intensive. The class is a combination of experience, lecture and discussion. You will have time to follow through the procedures of giving and receiving a Reiki Treatment using scanning, beaming and closure method. You will be learning
four symbols and how to use them in the Reiki work. We will be doing a Reiki meditation for empowering your gifts and talents. There is a closing crystal and ritual ceremony - an opportunity for you to share in healing of yourself, others, and the Planet.

It is recommended that you set aside time to practice about once a week for three months, or join together with a group of Reiki practitioners in your area - create your own Reiki Open House.

We have found the Reiki Open idea to be beneficial to ourselves, our friends and our community. We share Reiki energy and love once a month for mini-treatments. Working together in your community will help build your self confidence in your abilities and you will have reached out to help others.

Cost: $250.00

Reiki Quantum Level

This a one day intensive and was created for those wanting to further their education about Reiki and Healing Techniques. This class gives you all the tools of Reiki and experiences. A Tibetan Healing Technique and Attunement will be taught. There is a special Golden Light Alignment Attunement given for this level. Time to share, meditation, and closing crystal ceremony.

Cost: $200.00

Class Schedules:

The Reiki and Beyond Training Center teaches classes all over the USA, as well as in other countries. If you are interested in attending a class, contact the Center to see if a class is being held in your area. If you would like to sponsor a class, contact the Center for further information.

Reiki and Beyond III/Masters

This is a two day intensive and teaches you all the attunements and initiations into Reiki. Practice time and instruction is given for the attunement procedures. A Teachers Manual will be provided with easy instructions. A place to keep a record of your symbols, notes for your personal journaling, and meditations. We will be covering the mysteries of your personal evolvement, and an opportunity of understanding the Ray and Color energy you are working with. Getting in touch with an angelic guide for the healing work of Reiki and a Native American guide for your work with the planet. This class is a personal and powerful healing experience - the Going Beyond.

Cost: $600.00

Certification

Requirement of certification: Reiki Quantum Level
To have received Reiki I and II
(anyone who has received their training can advance into Reiki Quantum Level)

Requirement of certification: Reiki III/Masters
Reiki I and II - training from any Master Teacher
Reiki Quantum Level required - before taking Reiki III/Masters Class
A Teachers Manual is provided for this class.

Reiki and Beyond Newsletter

The newsletter contains healing experiences, a children's column, class schedules, networking information, and updates on planetary issues by noted psychics. Published quarterly: Subscription cost is $4.00 per year.

Reiki and Beyond Training Center
a non-profit organization
P.O. Box 1734
Virginia Beach, Virginia 23451
Tele: (804) 422-0087 (Va residents) or 1-800-892-0017 (out of state)

One Planet ♥♥♥♥♥ One People

Reiki and Beyond Training Center

A non-profit organization (Grassroots Research) was organized in 1994. Under this umbrella are the following:

- ♥ Reiki and Beyond Training Center
- ♥ Reiki and Beyond Newsletter
- ♥ Reiki Open House
- ♥ Bodywork Massage
- ♥ Great White Spirit Medicine Wheel
- ♥ Moon Lodge (Goddess Council)
- ♥ Workshops, Native American Art, and more

The Reiki training offered by the Center is based upon Dr. Usui and Dr. Hayashi's methods, and moves beyond for the needs of the community and the planet.

Our Board of Council:

- ♥ Minister and Counseling
- ♥ Elder teaching Native American customs
- ♥ Elder guiding visual healing and spiritual guidance
- ♥ Newsletter Staff
- ♥ Office and financial guidance director

Mystical experiences during the past few years have guided us toward opening the Center, and providing Reiki Training and guidance in healing. The Reiki Newsletter is our way of sending out networking information, healing experiences, stories for children, workshop schedules, and planetary updates - our own way of healing the One Planet ♥ One People, we want to be a part of the Rainbow Heart Connection.

Reiki and Beyond Training Center Fees

This Center has made fee changes for the Reiki classes to help make Reiki more affordable. Classes are available at the Center (check for dates) or you can sponsor a class in your area (please call to make arrangements).

Reiki I and II:	**$250.00**
Quantum Reiki:	**$200.00**
Reiki III/Master:	**$600.00**

THE CHALLENGE CONTINUES

The Thunder had come, the lightening too,
The command was given to just a few;
Out into the quadrants: earth, air, fire and sea
Gods calling out, and not just to me!

The Thunder People heard the decree,
To pass on the knowledge to you and to me;
From all directions, out into the universe, a start
Reaching out with the lessons of the Heart.

Whether white, black, yellow or red,
"The brotherhood of man is required", he said.
Reach out to your Guides and your Angels so Bright
Still your mind with God's purpose, become the Light.

The Rainbow Legacy - The Thunder - The Challenge - The Plan
All of us needing to be the best that we can.
Are we meeting the Challenge, following The Great Plan,
Or are we caught off guard, with our heads in the sand?

The Spirit Clan communicated with the Force
Beings beyond the Thunder in the rain clouds of course.
The ones who ride Star Vehicles creating sonic booms,
Are they waiting for acknowledgment too soon?

Oh Thunder People, the holy ones of the tribe
You who bring great truths, along with our Guides;
I acknowledge your power, your peace, and your force
I join you today, with my heart and spirit source!

Wind Dancer

My Angelic Experience

My story and why this book??!!

Time - Spring.   Place - New York area.
It was late one night and my plans to stay overnight had suddenly been changed.

Here I was put in the boonies with no place to stay and extremely tired. It had been a long trip to New York and a three day intensive and here I was just starting my long journey back home. Needless to say, when you are upset, one should try and get centered before getting into an automobile. I didn't.

I was traveling along this very hilly two lane winding road and saw lights up ahead where a vehicle was off to the side of the road, next to a house. Since I was still in an upset mood, I wasn't thinking of danger ahead.

Very soon my eyes saw the full panoramic view!! On my left a house and car sitting in the road, on the right a dead deer, a deep ditch and mountain coming down to meet the ditch. I knew immediately the way was blocked, there was no way through.

With a deep groan from within myself, I said, "Oh my God"! I hit the brakes immediately and lost control of my truck. I was aware of trying to maneuver the truck and keep from rolling over, struggling with the wheel feeling the rocking back and forth.

My next awareness was driving straight - down the road, tears already had welled up and run down to my chin. I saw no lights, nothing behind me, only a quiet and peacefulness. There were stars out and I heard myself saying, "Oh, what happened, I'm going straight. How could I possibly be going straight"?

Then sensing this intense urgency to look at the seat next to me, although I knew no one was riding with me; but I was impelled to look anyway. I saw this beautiful Angelic light and being; I heard myself softly whisper, "thank you, oh thank you". What was it: a time lapse, a space warp, a miracle!

My next cognizance was, "Well, you must have something left for me to do on this planet". Knowing that mercy and grace had been gifted to me. Again, only much louder and claiming the action, I said, "Tell me what it is, you want me to do, I will do it"!

A picture flashed before my eyes and I knew I was to put together a Healing Manual that would help others. A journey towards their personal pathway, just as I have been helped this night and over the years.

I am fulfilling my commitment, and loving the idea and opportunity of helping you and the planet to become the One Planet ♥ One People!

What a blessing, and what a way to be re-awoken!

Jeanne

One Planet ♥ ♥ ♥ ♥ ♥ One People

CRYSTAL CEREMONY

At the end of each workshop we will perform a crystal healing ceremony.
This ceremony is based on the Native American concept of the Medicine Wheel.

We will **call** in: Four Directions, the Four Archangels, the Four Elements, Power Animals

We will **send** out: Healing to the waters of the planet, to the peoples of the planet, to each other

We will **take part** in: Color energy, the rhythms of the earth and the spiral dance

We will **learn:** About sage, blessings, our connection, our purpose

Our ceremony will promote our goal . . . One Planet ♥ One People!

ABOUT THE AUTHOR:

Believer In Angels

Since birth Jeanne has been aware there is more to life than the material world. A believer in Angels and a sensitive, she became involved in Spiritual Evolvement over fifteen years ago. Her main interest has been working with the auras, fields of energy, meditation, massage work, healing and teaching.

Developer of Bodywork & Co. (therapeutic body massage). She promotes physical and spiritual health and healing; and shares her insights and understanding with others.

Since her near death Angel experience, she has devoted her time towards putting this Manual together. This manual is a product of knowledge and experiences by Jeanne and Friends. Thus the birth of: Reiki and Beyond Healing Manual - One Planet ♥ One People!

She is the founder of the Reiki and Beyond Training Center located in the Virginia Beach area; and Editor of the Reiki Newsletter.

Background: Therapeutic Bodywork Massage, Counselor, Minister, Channel,
Artist, Tarot, Astrology, Sacred Shields (Native American)
Reiki Master, Angelic Guidance, and Teaches various other workshops through:

- ♥ Focus of body, mind and spirit towards Infinity
- ♥ Guidance in discovering our direction and who are
- ♥ Moving beyond our fears and guilt
- ♥ Moving into unlimiting views, the quantum aspect
- ♥ A journey of love and understanding yourself

S. Jeanne Gunn, Quantum Reiki Master

One Planet ♥ ♥ ♥ ♥ ♥ One People

NOTES:

NOTES:

NOTES: